PSYCHOTHERAPY
WITH
COLLEGE
STUDENTS

Report No. 130

PSYCHOTHERAPY WITH COLLEGE STUDENTS

Formulated by the
Committee on the College Student

GROUP FOR THE ADVANCEMENT OF PSYCHIATRY

BRUNNER/MAZEL *Publishers* ● New York

Library of Congress Cataloging-in-Publication Data
Psychotherapy with college students / formulated by the Committee on
the College Student, Group for the Advancement of Psychiatry.
     p.   cm. -- (Report ; no. 130)
     Includes bibliographical references.
     ISBN 0-87630-613-X (hardcover). -- ISBN 0-87630-614-8 (pbk.)
     1. College students--Mental health.   2. Psychotherapy.   I. Group
for the Advancement of Psychiatry. Committee on the College
Student. II. Series: Report (Group for the Advancement of
Psychiatry : 1984) ; no. 130.
     [DNLM: 1. Psychotherapy. 2. Student Health Services. 3. Student-
-psychology.   W1 RE209BR no. 130 / WA 353 P974]
RC321.G7 no. 130
616.89 s--dc20
[616.89'14'0088375]
DNLM/DLC
for Library of Congress   90-2345
                                                                  CIP

Published by
BRUNNER/MAZEL, INC.
19 Union Square West
New York, New York, 10003

Manufactured in the United States of America

10 9 8 7 6 5 4 3 2 1

STATEMENT OF PURPOSE

THE GROUP FOR THE ADVANCEMENT OF PSYCHIATRY has a membership of approximately 300 psychiatrists, most of whom are organized in the form of a number of working committees. These committees direct their efforts toward the study of various aspects of psychiatry and the application of this knowledge to the fields of mental health and human relations.

Collaboration with specialists in other disciplines has been and is one of GAP's working principles. Since the formation of GAP in 1946, its members have worked closely with such other specialists as anthropologists, biologists, economists, statisticians, educators, lawyers, nurses, psychologists, sociologists, social workers, and experts in mass communication, philosophy, and semantics. GAP envisages a continuing program of work according to the following aims:

1. To collect and appraise significant data in the fields of psychiatry, mental health, and human relations;
2. To reevaluate old concepts and to develop and test new ones;
3. To apply the knowledge thus obtained for the promotion of mental health and good human relations.

GAP is an independent group, and its reports represent the composite findings and opinions of its members only, guided by its many consultants.

Psychotherapy with College Students was formulated by the Committee on the College Student. The members of this committee are listed on page vii. The members of the other GAP committees, as well as additional membership categories and current and past officers of GAP, are listed at the end of the report.

v

This report is dedicated to Kent E. Robinson, M.D., and Joseph Katz, Ph.D., who worked on this report until their deaths. Dr. Robinson, a long-time GAP member, was Chairman of our Committee during the drafting of this report. Dr. Katz served as a consultant to our Committee for many years.

CONTENTS

PSYCHOTHERAPY
WITH
COLLEGE STUDENTS

1

PREAMBLE

In the early 1950s, David enrolled at a prestigious college expecting to become an English major and go into journalism. He tried out for the college newspaper, but spent so much time at this extracurricular work that by February he was in danger of flunking out. Depressed and anxious, he was sent by his advisor to see the psychiatrist at the Student Mental Health Service.

The psychiatrist asked David why he was working so hard on the paper that he could not get his studies done. He responded that his mother had told him that extracurricular activities were important. She worked in advertising and wanted him to be an English major and to familiarize himself with newspaper work. When David was asked what *he* thought was important, he replied that he guessed that he agreed with his mother. The psychiatrist ended the first interview by telling David that he really ought to be giving some thought to what he was interested in doing with his life.

David opened the second interview by expressing a good deal of anger toward the psychiatrist because he believed that he had already given a lot of thought to what he wanted to do with his life. He had always wanted to be an engineer like his father. Throughout high school, he and his father had built rockets and made expeditions to the country to set them off. But his mother had depreciated this activity, and his father had failed to encourage his engineering interests.

During his senior year of high school he had been sent to a therapist because he was somewhat shy and had trouble making friends. This therapist had interpreted the rockets he and his father built to be "phallic symbols," further undermining these interests as real career possibilities. The psychiatrist's comment to this information was, "So you have thought a great deal about whether or not other people have encouraged you in what you want to do, but I'm still not sure that you have thought enough about what you really want to do."

The second appointment had come before spring break, and David remembers feeling furious, first with his doctor, then with himself, and finally with his mother and father. He went home for spring break determined to confront his parents about what he wanted to do about college. He did so, and to his surprise, his mother did not force her view, and his father was pleased and encouraging.

He canceled a third appointment scheduled for after the spring break, because he did not feel a need for more visits. The next fall he enrolled in an engineering college to pursue a degree in engineering.

David entered psychotherapy 30 years later because of marital problems. At that time, he held a high position with a government agency. Professionally, he was extremely successful and happy, and he reported that since college, his life had been relatively untroubled.

In one session early in treatment, David reminisced about how happy and productive he had been as an engineer, and how close he had come to missing this happiness. He gave his two brief psychiatric visits while in college credit for having helped him make the right decision.

This man did a remarkable amount of work in the very brief therapy in college. He was able successfully to consolidate the career aspects of his identity for the rest of his life to that point, but obviously not everything was resolved in such a brief therapy. His marriage was characterized by chronic resentment toward his wife, whom he saw as continually trying to dominate and control him—a repetition of his adolescent conflict with his mother. In addition, he worried that he really did not know how to be a father to his children. Resolving these issues required a fairly long and more intensive course of psychotherapy. After three years of treatment, David ruefully said that if he had only spent three more sessions as a freshman, he might not have had to spend three years in therapy as an adult.

While we believe that there is some truth in his obviously somewhat facetious statement, in fact, he had not been ready for extensive therapy in college. At that time, he only needed help with developmental tasks related to his freshman year experiences. He repeated, in part, his parental conflict with his therapist and needed to distance himself in order to insure his feeling of autonomy and to let him take charge of his own life in new and important ways.

This report will attempt to clarify how and why such useful therapeutic work often gets accomplished in short courses of psychotherapy with college students.

2

INTRODUCTION

The kind of therapeutic interaction described in the Preamble is familiar to anyone who has worked in a college mental health center. Undergraduates most often present for treatment when they are feeling acutely troubled by a current problem or situation. They come for a relatively brief treatment experience, which one hopes will help either resolve the situation or give sufficient insight about the problem or conflict that barriers to spontaneous growth are removed and they are better able to cope. They may accomplish a great deal, even though much remains unexplored. They leave feeling better, and may or may not come back with future problems, but they seldom settle into long-term psychotherapy.* The better we, as therapists, can understand the life struggles and inner world of college students, the more we can help them in therapy.

The Committee on the College Student has written several reports regarding college mental health issues, which may serve as a useful background for this report (GAP, 1965, 1975, 1983). This report is written primarily for professionals who are engaged in psychotherapy with undergraduate college students in a campus setting or in private practice, or who are supervising those who are. It will not attempt to describe or discuss the varied roles—consultative, preventive, educative, administrative—that the psychiatrist on campus may be asked

---

*We are talking primarily about undergraduates with problems relating to development. Inevitably, a number of students will suffer from neurotic syndromes or character disorders that will require longer term psychotherapy, and possibly pharmacotherapy as well.

to fill. Although these are vital activities and may occupy much of a campus psychiatrist's time, this report will be restricted to the narrower psychotherapeutic task.

College students are not merely adolescents who happen to have entered college, nor are they adults who just happen to have not yet finished school; they are adolescents who are in the process of becoming young adults.* This transition period is one in which the individual is especially vulnerable, and subject to a variety of impulsive behaviors as well as intense feelings in the process of forming an identity and achieving adulthood. The college experience may be viewed as a modern rite of passage for those who attend. This report will examine the special and unique psychotherapeutic issues involved in treating this group of individuals, and it will attempt to explicate how these issues affect the therapeutic process.

Our experience has shown that over the years, the average number of visits to mental health services by students seeking help has been 4 to 5 (Reifler & Liptzin, 1969; Schwartz & Reifler, 1984). This figure has held steady for many years, and continues to hold true even in mental health services that offer unlimited visits. Follow-up studies indicate that this brevity of treatment is not a sign of student dissatisfaction with the available mental health services (Dorosin et al., 1976; Haggerty et al., 1980). In our discussions with colleagues at university health services, and from data collected by the American College Health Association Mental Health Annual Program Surveys we find that even in those settings where the university does not explicitly impose restrictions on the number of visits, the average number of visits by all users of the service is not appreciably greater. Professionals in private practice also report that much can be done to help students in relatively few visits.

---

*Although we recognize that many college students now are older, our report will focus generally on the traditional college ages of 17–22. In Chapter 5 we will discuss some aspects of older students returning to college. Our focus does not include graduate or professional students, who may present with some of the same problems, but who are at a different place in their lives.

We believe that carrying out psychotherapy with college students is most effective if one understands the developmental tasks of late adolescence and how these tasks are interwoven into the college experience, including their relationship to the institutional and academic setting within which students live and work. For many therapists who work on college campuses, the section of our report dealing with the institutional setting may be familiar. For some who have worked on campuses in the past but have gone on to other settings, the section may be a useful reminder of what the student encounters in academic life. For those who have college students as patients in therapy and rarely think about or pay attention to what is going on in the student's college life, we hope that this orientation will add an important conceptual dimension.

We have found that undergraduates most often seek consultation or treatment when an event or experience touches or evokes a psychological conflict occurring within the context of a developmental struggle of late adolescence. This conflict reflects a clash between the intrapsychic developmental needs of students, their unresolved past experiences with earlier editions of similar conflicts, the real or perceived needs in their current lives (including those expectations expressed by their parents), and pressures inherent in the institutional or academic requirements of the college. When these disparate needs, expectations, and requirements are in a state of equilibrium, a student's emotional life is likely to be relatively calm. When disequilibrium and conflict occur, the student is likely to be anxious, depressed, and in turmoil.

In the case described in the Preamble, David came to treatment at the height of a conflict that developed in his freshman year. While he was meeting his mother's expectations by planning to major in English and by engaging in literary and extracurricular activities, he was simultaneously failing to progress in the normal adolescent developmental task of establishing appropriate autonomy in relation to his parents. Unconsciously, he was undermining his mother's plan by neglecting his studies and arranging to flunk out of the college she had chosen for him. Although this attempt at resolution could be seen as his expressing a wish for greater self-sufficiency, it was also self-defeating and brought him into direct conflict with a requirement of the college. It is difficult to predict the long range repercussions if he had actually failed; at the least, it would have produced an unnecessary and painful disruption in his life.

His presenting problem suggested a self-defeating allocation of time and energy between his academic and extracurricular work, with his choice having implications for his career. More fundamental, however, was the fact that he needed help in his struggle with the developmentally determined changing relationship with his parents, particularly, in this instance, with his mother. In the first interview, his psychiatrist emphasized this point by asking David what it was *he* thought was important, and what *he* was interested in doing with his life. The emphasis, thus, was not narrowly focused on the current crisis or even on future career or work identity, but rather on David as a person, separate from others including his parents. The psychiatrist recognized the importance of helping this freshman to begin to take more responsibility for his own decisions so that he could move forward in his personal development. In the second meeting, the psychiatrist again focused on this task by noting that David was still not addressing the issue of what *he* really wanted to do. When this new authority figure asked a few pointed questions, David became aware of his resentment toward his mother, which he was unconsciously expressing by flunking out of college.

It is somewhat paradoxical that David's anger was initially directed toward the psychiatrist. This can be understood as a manifestation of a transference reaction; that is, he was reliving or experiencing in his relationship with his therapist feelings similar to those that had existed in earlier experiences with his parents. He was really angry at them for encouraging his continuing dependence, and perhaps for not adequately fostering his autonomy and personal development. After coming to understand more clearly the actual target of his anger, he went home for spring break and was able to confront his parents in a discussion of what *he* wanted to do, including transferring to another college of *his* choice. We assume that David was then able to begin to integrate his identification with his father and his own proven interests in engineering so that a more solid and satisfactory work identity could result.

As noted in this brief vignette, developmental issues may seem to have been resolved earlier in adolescence, only to reappear in college to be reworked and further consolidated. Often, such consolidation can be assisted by brief psychotherapy. In this report, we will use current psychodynamic theories of personality development to understand the maturational events that bring students into treatment.

This report emphasizes that, whatever the particular form of therapy, students tend to benefit from treatment when they can attain a better understanding of the interplay of their life situation at college, their ongoing relationships with family and peers, and past, unresolved internal conflicts that have adversely affected normal developmental progression (GAP, 1983).

Does psychotherapy with college students really differ from psychotherapy with adults? The most accurate answer is "yes and no." In many respects it is similar, but we will try to identify unique factors that we believe must be taken into account if the therapy is to be most effective. Many therapists believe that college students are ideal subjects for psychotherapeutic work since they are usually verbal, are often occupied with self-exploration, and their psychological structure is still quite fluid. Details of early life experiences often are surprisingly accessible, and insight may lead to remarkable gains.

Earlier developmental conflicts normally appear in late adolescence. This, combined with strivings for autonomy and newly developed capacities for self-awareness, constitutes a remarkable opportunity for change through psychotherapy. In the process of separating from family, college students who turn to other adults for help in solving psychological problems are already taking a significant developmental step. A therapist who helps students explore their current conflicts and arrive at new solutions can have an enormous impact on their growth. It is usually unnecessary to explore in great detail early childhood experiences. However, it is important to allow and sometimes to foster the appearance of older editions of the current problems. In this way new solutions to the original problems can be included in the treatment, thereby enriching and validating the totality of the current therapy as well as providing an additional level of understanding and accomplishment that will help the student cope more effectively with similar problems in the future.

The kind of therapy that is offered depends on the problems that the student presents, the orientation and experience of the therapist, and the availability of therapeutic resources within the institution or outside. Most colleges these days have a small number of therapists with a limited number of hours. Thus, the help offered on campus is likely to be of short duration, but if further therapy is necessary, referrals can sometimes be made to outside therapists.

Therapists must know about the student's academic situation. College students are enrolled in an educational institution, and while that does not change the fundamental principles that guide psychotherapy, it does indicate that education is an essential part of their lives and an appropriate subject of the therapeutic inquiry. This does not mean that the therapist should be directive, but it does mean that there are times when providing or eliciting facts can be helpful. Students usually will share information when asked about the courses that they are taking, how well they are doing, and the relative importance of each course. In the presence of specific academic blocks that have not responded to reasonable corrective efforts, it is essential to consider them as possible manifestations of some unexplored psychological problem. If a student is doing poorly in a particular course, exploration of the course and its specific content can be psychodynamically revealing, as may exploration of the student's relationship with the teacher. Students may defensively deflect attention away from academic problems and focus on relationships or other areas (GAP, 1983). However, it is counterproductive (as well as embarrassing) after a semester's work on "relationship problems" for a therapist to find that the student has flunked out of school without ever having mentioned academic difficulties during treatment. Withdrawal from school may actually be a positive move, but flunking out is not necessarily the best way to manage it. At the least, some discussion of the event beforehand seems appropriate. Similarly, a student may be heavily involved in using drugs or drinking excessively and not mention these facts in coming to a therapist.

This report focuses on psychodynamically oriented psychotherapy, based conceptually on psychoanalytic principles. Although experienced therapists will find the ensuing description of psychotherapy principles and technique elementary, we are including it for the clarification of our therapeutic premises and, perhaps, as an aid to less experienced therapists.

Our underlying assumptions characterizing psychodynamic psychotherapy include the following principles:

1) Intrapsychic events and conflicts are important in determining normal and pathological development. We listen and look carefully beyond the presenting complaints or behaviors in order to understand more fully.

2) Unconscious mental processes exist and significantly affect mental functioning. This means that certain ideas, wishes, feelings, and memories, not consciously available to the individual, are not simply forgotten, but in fact are actively and purposefully kept out of awareness. At the same time, they are powerful motivators and contributors to conflict and behavior. Therapists do not have direct access to these processes but can infer their existence by paying attention to the student's behavior, dreams, associations, and affective responses in the therapy sessions.

3) An individual's current problems are usually historically related to earlier conflictual experiences that may not be

known consciously. Thus, causal connections exist between these earlier experiences and current conflicts, and the former may be major determinants, although the latter are often perceived as if they were the result of current circumstances alone.

4) Therapeutic change is achieved in a number of ways. The therapist helps the individual make sense of current feelings and behavior. When possible, this understanding is connected to early experiences. In order to be helpful, these connections must be linked on an emotional feeling level, not merely understood as intellectual ideas.

5) There are certain characteristic repetitive patterns in the lives of people that derive from early formative experiences, and often underlie the difficulties in important current relationships. These patterns and associated feelings will be repeated in part in the student's relationship with the therapist. This special interaction that occurs in therapy is technically known as transference. Both the student and the therapist may participate, without being aware of it, in recreating these patterns. The student carries over these images from the past and projects them onto the therapist. Similarly, the therapist may respond in an unconscious way stemming from the therapist's own early experience; this response is referred to as countertransference. The therapist's observations of transference and countertransference patterns can be used in the treatment to explore and understand the student's current interpersonal problems.

In addition to the underlying principles of psychodynamic psychotherapy, there are certain factors that make the psychotherapeutic relationship unique and that contribute to the curative effect.

1) The therapist listens. Listening with the aim of understanding is in itself helpful. It conveys concern and a focus on the student, with attention to feelings and to recognizing repeated patterns of reaction and behavior. Furthermore,

through understanding and interpretation, the therapist offers the possibility for new ways of coping with conflicts.

The act of verbalizing feelings and concerns is in itself an important process, one that permits some objective review of emotionally charged recollections. Talking about and reflecting on intensely felt issues provides perspective and conveys the idea that behavior, feelings, and concerns can be understood and formulated in terms of cause and effect. Sometimes, just the process of labeling a reaction or behavior is a step toward mastery. It establishes the fact that this feeling or problem exists, that other people experience it, and that it is not simply a secret issue for the patient alone. It reduces defensiveness so that exploratory treatment can proceed more readily along lines of psychological causality.

Catharsis, the relief of expressing emotion or "getting something off one's chest," may also be beneficial. Catharsis could occur in a nonpsychotherapeutic context, for example, in a heart-to-heart talk with a good friend or relative, but under such circumstances, the student may be reluctant or embarrassed to confide in full for fear that disclosure will compromise the relationship. The psychotherapeutic situation is different in that any complications arising from the disclosure can be dealt with as meaningful components of the treatment. Moreover, the therapist has the ability to go beyond catharsis and help achieve a greater depth of understanding about the origins and causes of the previously unacknowledged or repressed emotions and thoughts.

2) Therapists remain neutral in attitude. This does not mean impassive, uncaring, or uninvolved, but neutral in the sense of not interjecting or imposing their own ideas, preferences, or attitudes about matters with which the student is struggling.

Therapists remain nonjudgmental and ally themselves primarily with the patient's attempts to reach solutions. At times this may be difficult, because the student may mention behaviors that worry the therapist, or that stir up certain protective or parental attitudes. For example, the student may be considering an unconventional stance or behavior with which the therapist disagrees or regards as not in the patient's interests, for example, precipitously dropping out of school. At such a juncture the therapist's task is to be aware of his or her own feelings and to remain the ally of the student in attempting to clarify the student's motivations. Usually, therapeutic neutrality also means that it is inappropriate to talk about the therapist's own personal experience. Thus, this controlled and unilateral relationship differs markedly from an ordinary friendship and from certain kinds of supportive therapy; it frees the student to talk without being distracted by the therapist's reactions.

3) The therapist points out patterns in the student's responses and behaviors and may link present problems or feelings with past experiences or events. Although they may seem very convincing to the therapist and patient, these are inferences initially. Their validity can be confirmed by subsequent information obtained from the treatment interaction, including the student's reactions to the therapist's comments. These can be considered clarifications, or even interpretations, although the term "interpretation" is often reserved for a comment that includes an element in the student's unconscious; it is rare, however, to obtain that depth of information in brief therapy. Occasionally, however, a behavior can be readily recognized as having an unconscious component, for example, repeatedly forgetting a particular class or losing an item of clothing associated with an old boyfriend or girlfriend. These are typically the result of significant ambivalences about the activity or relationship. An accurate interpretation can increase conscious understanding and result in more effective ways of dealing with the newly perceived problem.

4) At times the therapist may directly question and confront the student to underline the potential risks or dangers that the student is courting by specific behavior in a given situation. A common current example is the reporting of sexual behavior that fails to acknowledge the possibility of contract-

ing an HIV infection. However, it is important to make every effort to keep the intervention in the usual format of exploratory inquiry. For example, one might inquire about the apparent absence of consideration of possible adverse outcomes or ask whether alternative solutions to the specific situation had been considered. The continued fostering of self-inquiry about important decisions or actions helps keep the focus on the student's responsibility for behavior. The enhancement of self-reliance and autonomy within the therapeutic experience is of utmost importance in this developmental period.

Sometimes the therapist is the only person to whom the patient has talked about certain personal issues and, therefore, the only person who can guide the student to sources of information or help, such as for academic or contraceptive counseling. Again this can be done in the context of therapy by inquiring if the student has tried to search out the appropriate resources on campus. The absence of such effort on the student's part can be a focus for therapeutic exploration, even as the necessary information is simultaneously offered.

5) Therapists must respect the concerns of the patient and not impose their own therapeutic ambitions; they must always remember that the therapeutic relationship is not a social one. Creating an atmosphere of trust, confidentiality, and safety is of extreme importance.

6) Confidentiality is crucial in a college environment. The therapist may be only one of several individuals attempting to help the student. When a student's behavior becomes annoying to other students, or disruptive, other authorities may become involved. The therapist may be approached for advice, exhorted to make the student change the offending behavior, or asked to reveal information about the student. It is important for the therapist to respond to such pressures carefully, so as to maintain a therapeutic role with the student that ensures confidentiality. Since students are constantly in situations where they are being evaluated, they

inevitably worry that involvement in therapy will somehow result in an adverse evaluation or be used against them; therefore, confidentiality is absolutely essential. Any breach thereof, real or imagined, will be disastrous to treatment.

Students are exquisitely sensitive to blurring of roles and to direct or indirect pressure to conform to the expectations of others, especially those in authority. They may misunderstand the therapist's pressure as a betrayal; consequently, they may either stop treatment or lose trust in the therapist. It is, therefore, essential for a therapist working in a student health center to clearly separate the role of advisor to administration from the role of therapist. This may require resisting all requests from administrative authorities, but must be balanced against alienating such authorities who are also in a helping role. It is usually possible to help the dean understand a specific problem or situation by a general discussion without reference to any particular individual. With this understanding, the dean may then feel more confident in taking appropriate administrative action (Blaine, 1964; Mooreman et al., 1984).

To reiterate our basic assumption, while long-term intensive therapy may sometimes be indicated as the treatment of choice for some students, for many students this may run counter to the thrust away from dependency and toward self-reliance characteristic of this developmental period. Brief therapeutic work focused primarily on the current active struggles of the student may be all that is needed at that time. As with the case of David cited in the Preamble, sometimes longer term treatment may also be indicated at a later stage of life.

3

TYPICAL PRESENTING PROBLEMS

College students present with a wide range of clinical syndromes. This chapter describes some of the most frequent and typical presenting concerns.

ACADEMIC PROBLEMS

The "work" for students in college is studying, learning, and demonstrating achievement by writing papers and exams. Difficulty with this work is one of the most common presenting concerns at a mental health service. Students experience several symptom patterns, including loss of interest in studying, difficulty concentrating, or blocks to learning. Students will seek help, infrequently, for examination panic and, not so infrequently, for inability to complete papers. In the early years of college, a fear of being intellectually incapable of doing the work may emerge, or anxiety about how to go about studying and learning. Treatment focusing on the feelings of inadequacy and anxiety will be helpful at this time. When specific study problems are involved, simultaneous remedial help may be indicated.

Our clinical experience suggests that one common underlying diagnosis for these various complaints is a clinical depression, with difficulty in learning or performance inhibition often the predominant symptoms. Difficulty in learning can also be the presenting symptom for life crises such as illness, psychosis, death in the family, or breakup of an important relationship.

In short, almost any crisis in the student's nonacademic life can result in difficulty in learning. Substance abuse, particularly alcohol, may be involved. When the student, by dint of seeking psychological help, identifies the learning problem as primarily psychological, it is essential to explore thoroughly all possible factors that may contribute to the difficulty.

Anxiety about grades is a common concern. Students worry that they are not achieving good enough grades to be accepted at competitive graduate programs. Such anxiety may also occur in relation to parental expectations, real or imagined, or to the student's own standards. Many college students have been at the top of their class in high school and have never before had to face the kind of competition they encounter in college. The first failure or the first time that they receive a grade lower than an A can be very traumatic; it can shatter their self-image and lead to embarrassment and confusion.

Being questioned, tested, and graded on examinations, and having their thoughts and ideas criticized can cause significant anxiety. The process can evoke unconscious residues; the experience of being questioned can reactivate old feelings of guilt; exposing ideas in papers can elicit feelings of inadequacy; and being examined and graded can be linked with past examinations, both physical and mental. Thus, earlier feelings of being found wanting and previous concerns with body image can make examinations seem inordinately hazardous.

Difficulty with writing papers and completing written assignments on time is a common concern. College may be the first setting in which formal papers are required, and the standards and expectations are different from those in high school. Some students are perfectionistic and unable to complete a paper because it does not meet their internally generated exacting standard. In addition, students may be reluctant to reveal their fantasized "true" selves with all their imperfections and inadequacies. Common feelings are: "If they see what I am really like, they will know they made a mistake in admitting me," or "They will see the really awful, fraudulent things I do."

Derek was a senior who withdrew for academic reasons because of an inability to complete papers. He came from a comfortable background with concerned and supportive parents. He spent a year working in a job he enjoyed and was readmitted in order to finish his degree. He continued to have difficulty and again ended the year short of credits because of uncompleted papers. Since he had only two credits to go, he was allowed to attend summer school. He came to therapy at the urging of his parents. He did not seem depressed or anxious. He presented as a young man with clear career goals and an enjoyable social life, who was unable to finish his papers because he wanted to do outstanding work. The need to turn in papers in order to graduate was not sufficient to overcome his writing inhibition without help.

In this case, the underlying problem had to do with the student's perfectionistic standards. His inhibition protected him from his anticipated sense of failure in relation to his exaggerated expectations of himself. His problem might also have derived from some other unconscious conflict, perhaps an area of inadequacy that he protected himself from thinking about by displacing the worry onto the writing inhibition. In therapy, Derek was able to focus on the specific goal of completing acceptable work to turn in. Cognitive therapy was directed at his all-or-nothing approach to tasks. He was instructed to keep a diary of his automatic negative thoughts. This enabled him to appreciate the irrational nature of his preoccupations, which, in his fantasies, typically resulted in dire consequences. His success at being able to work productively according to a schedule he set for himself, rather than to lapse into reveries of hopeless despair, bolstered his confidence. In addition, he arranged regular meetings with his sympathetic professor to review his progress, further keeping him on track (Burns et al., 1987).

Other problems in intellectual or artistic endeavors frequently relate to unconscious conflicts pertaining to sexual adequacy or creativity.

Students often complain of difficulty concentrating and

learning. As noted, this is frequently a manifestation of anxiety, depression, or preoccupation with other concerns. More rarely, it results from realistic problems such as noise in the dorms. At times, difficulty in concentration is a sign of intense ambivalence about career directions.

> Larry, the youngest of four children, and his parents' only son, was seen in the fall semester of his senior year because of work inhibition. He was required to hand in a first draft of his senior essay by the following January in order to graduate. He was attempting to write a "Nobel Prize" paper on James Joyce. He had been brought up to believe that he must become either a doctor or lawyer to make up for his parents' disappointment in their daughters. He had incorporated these parental expectations and found it impossible to consider a career in English literature to which, in fact, he had made a considerable commitment and which he found quite fascinating. He had absolutely no interest in law and very little in medicine. Whenever he related one of his successes in English to his parents, their response was always, "That is very nice but when are you going to apply to law school?" When faced with his senior essay, he found himself paralyzed, able neither to complete his work nor to choose a future course of study.

Treatment for this presenting problem would certainly focus initially· on exploring his inability, even as a senior, to talk directly with his parents about himself and his own wishes, future interests, and career goals. Problems in identity are suggested.

A few students who present with concerns about academic problems may actually have learning disabilities. They experience great difficulty in organizing information and can benefit from special tutoring. This condition should be considered when there is a history of unusual difficulty in acquiring a new language (Freed, 1987; Gajar, 1987). Therapists should be aware that a learning disability may present as anxiety or depression, because the students are genuinely confused by their inability to keep up with college-level work when they have successfully managed high school. Some learning disabilities are quite subtle and may not become apparent until the students are confronted with college-level tasks. Some colleges employ specialists to perform diagnostic testing and to provide behavioral treatments for these students (Faigel, 1985; Miller & Cabell, 1989).

SEPARATION PROBLEMS

Separation from the family is a developmental task that usually occurs during late adolescence (see Chapter 4), and difficulties with separation are often a reason for seeking help. These occur most frequently in the freshman year, but may continue throughout college or surface initially later on. The residential student may be preoccupied with thoughts about parents and family and feel a need for frequent contact through letters, telephone calls, and visits. The student may identify this combination as homesickness, which can be mild or intense. The commuting student's separation problem may be more disguised and expressed in symptoms such as depression, irritability, insomnia, and inability to concentrate. Homesickness may result from the shock of being on one's own in a large unfamiliar residential college, or from worrying about what is happening to the family at home. Sometimes the latter worry is an expression of loneliness and difficulty in leaving the familiar home environment; at other times it is an intuitive feeling that all is not well at home—a feeling that may be accurate. Thus, the process of separation may be further complicated at this time if family problems such as parental illness, divorce, or separation occur. Parental separation may actually be more frequent than one might suppose; after years of estrangement, parents may have waited until children leave home before implementing a separation or filing for divorce, believing that this timing will be less traumatic for the children. They may not realize that in the process of developing independence and separation from parents and home, the adolescent is particularly sensitive and responsive to family instability.

Although experiencing some distressing anxieties initially, Joan thought she had made the transition to her freshman year at college successfully. She had begun to enjoy dorm life and was running for social chair. Classes were going well. She became upset, however, when she received a letter from home the week after Christmas break saying that her parents had separated and were planning to be divorced. Initially jolted and totally "surprised," Joan sought therapy, and, in therapy, realized that one of her anxieties early in freshman year had been a vague feeling that she should have stayed home "to save her parents' marriage." This made no logical sense to her at the time, but her mother told her later that her father had been having a long-term affair. The decision to divorce had been made some time before, but they had delayed telling Joan until all details had been settled.

Therapy sessions helped Joan to refocus on her own life and to reduce her preoccupation with assuming an inappropriate role at home.

At times going away to college can reactivate feelings of grief about the earlier death of a parent. The ensuing reaction can be overwhelming, especially if it is the student's first such experience of death.

Tom, a freshman, came to the mental health service saying that he couldn't accept anything less than A's and complaining that his father felt the same way. As Tom talked about his life, he revealed that his mother had died of cancer the year before after an illness of almost a year. During her illness and after her death, he coped with his grief by staying away from home, studying, and participating in every available sport and extracurricular activity. He tried to do the same in college, but it did not seem to work.

The therapist noted that Tom had not allowed himself to feel all of his painful feelings and that he had used studying as a means of protecting himself. Not only were studying and grieving difficult to do together, but for him studying had become a way to avoid thinking about his mother. Later therapeutic work showed that his father had reinforced the earlier incomplete mourning because of his need to curtail his own mourning. It was the separation from his father that allowed the student's previously repressed feelings to reemerge at this time.

Separation and homesickness are usually related, but separation problems may not be resolved as easily, and the student may continue to struggle with them after homesickness has essentially disappeared. Conversely, very severe homesickness may actually be symptomatic of more serious psychopathology, and may require a more aggressive therapeutic response, perhaps involving medication.

HOUSING PROBLEMS

Another important and sometimes hidden area of difficulty for residential students involves problems with roommates. Rooming problems may be difficult to resolve because a room change may not be possible, and other alternatives do not always exist.

> George, an 18-year-old college freshman, came to the mental health service just prior to midterm exams. He complained of problems adjusting to his college roommate who was inconsiderately keeping him awake well past his usual bedtime by studying late while playing his stereo loudly. George had discussed his dilemma with the residence hall staff hoping for a room change, but this couldn't be arranged. He was encouraged to try to work out these differences with his roommate, and he was beginning to be more optimistic about his living situation, although somewhat frantic about his studies as a result of the diversion of his energies.
>
> This common complaint, which troubles many freshmen, was complicated by the fact that George was diabetic, and during the several weeks of impasse and negotiation with his roommate, he had begun to drink beer and wine excessively at bedtime in order to help himself fall asleep. His diabetes, which had been well managed with insulin, was now out of control, so that his health was affected, and required close

medical monitoring. After George consulted his academic adviser, his best judgment was that he was too far behind to pass midterms, or hope to catch up and do well for the remainder of the semester. The Dean recommended that George drop out of school and get a fresh start next semester. At George's request, his therapist was able to recommend medical withdrawal, and to support his request for a single dorm room when he returned.

Particularly during the freshman year, roommates are often assigned randomly by a housing office so that there is a large element of chance in the ensuing degree of compatibility. In subsequent years roommates are likely to be self-chosen and, therefore, better matched, but even then, rooming together uncovers irritations that friendship did not. In addition to incompatibility, small rooms and crowded conditions increase tensions.

Terri, a 19-year-old college freshman, presented for counseling as a somewhat immature looking young woman. She dressed in typical college casuals, but she managed to look more disheveled and childish than one might expect. She complained of being overwhelmed by a combination of roommate problems, sorority rushing, falling grades, and fears of disappointing her parents. "I think," she said, "that I'm going crazy." She appeared deeply agitated and scattered. In the first hour it was difficult to help her identify a primary issue around which brief therapy could focus and substantive clarifications could be made. It finally emerged that she was in acute distress about her relationship with her roommate, which seemed to the therapist to be bordering on becoming overtly sexual. The most conscious issue between the two women was that Terri felt a subservience to the roommate, whom she perceived to be more mature, independent, and sophisticated. In return for her adoration and obedience, Terri expected an unrealistic level of intense involvement, comfort, understanding, and definition. She felt enraged and/or jealous when these attentions were in any way withdrawn, for example when the roommate started dating. (This case is discussed further in Chapter 6.)

This vignette illustrates the complications that can occur in rooming relationships. Here, the two students were not incompatible, but they had interlocking personality patterns that created different needs and, consequently, considerable distress.

RELATIONSHIP PROBLEMS

Many students seek help involving current relationships with roommates, friends, or lovers (GAP, 1983). Relationship problems need to be explored dynamically. Past problems with siblings frequently come to the fore. There can also be difficulties with the lack of privacy in dormitory rooms; in particular, exposure to a roommate's sexual activity may generate considerable upset.

> Ben's freshman roommate ostentatiously made clear that he was a "stud" by displaying a variety of condoms with comments on his preference. Although Ben felt that most of this might be talk, on the second Saturday of the semester he returned from the movies to find a sign on their door: Keep Out, Man at Work! Ben waited and as time passed became more upset. When the roommate finally emerged, the two of them got into a shouting match. Ben decided to seek therapy for help with his recurrent feelings of inadequacy. During the first session he talked of his past troubled relationship with an older brother. The therapist helped him to understand that although anyone might be upset by the inconsiderateness of the roommate, the fact that Ben had an older brother who had frequently belittled Ben's abilities with girls while boasting about his own sexual prowess intensified Ben's reaction to the situation.

Sexual relationships and problems associated with them are important sources of stress for students (GAP, 1965). The breaking up of a relationship can be extremely painful, especially if one of the students feels isolated from familiar supports in their joint circle of friends. How to make decisions about sexuality, and what influences such decisions are also matters of concern.

> Linda, a 20-year-old junior, was seen at the mental health service because of "problems with my boyfriend." She had a steady boyfriend named Joe, to whom she felt committed. She was bothered by his being somewhat constricted and obsessive but felt that she was in love with him. Several months before she came to the clinic she had been working many hours on the student newspaper with Bob, who was the boyfriend of her best girlfriend. After working together for several months, Linda and Bob had begun to have intercourse, and she felt terribly guilty about this, in terms of how this would affect both Joe and her girlfriend. In describing the situation initially, she started to reflect on why she and Bob had decided to have intercourse together. She realized that it was something that they had really not decided but had just drifted into. For her part, she had assumed that it was expected of her, given the new sexual freedom that women now enjoy, and yet she became quite upset as a result. (This case is discussed further in Chapter 6.)

Sometimes separation, housing, and relationship (or lack thereof) problems all interact as the following vignette illustrates.

> Tim, an 18-year-old freshman, came to the mental health clinic with complaints of loneliness and depression. He lived in a neighboring town some 40 miles distant, and had been visiting home about every three weeks. He had been active in high school and friendly with Randy and Carol, who were dating. The three of them did many things together, and he often confided in Randy about personal concerns. He and Randy decided to room together in college. Once at college, he was quite surprised and disappointed that he no longer felt as close to Randy and felt less able to confide in him. He wondered whether it was because Randy and Carol were spending more time alone together.

About two weeks before Tim came for help, he stayed in the lounge until 3:00 a.m. while Randy and Carol were in the room together. He felt quite annoyed but didn't say anything. Although he didn't think that Randy and Carol were sexually intimate, the thought occurred to him, and one week before coming in, he made a "joking" remark to Carol asking her "how her sex life was." She seemed quite irritated by this remark and did not speak to him for four days. Neither he nor Randy mentioned it.

Generally, he was having trouble in his adjustment to college. His parents had separated for a brief period three years ago, and on the occasions when he went home, he became uneasy when his parents began to argue. He had not been attending church since coming to school and felt the need to do so. He had started playing racquetball several times a week with some new acquaintances in the dorm, and he enjoyed this, but he was able to say in the initial session that he felt lonely and very much wanted to date a girl and have some sexual experience. In high school, he dated only one classmate for a brief period of time. They were not seriously involved, and he ended the relationship. He had tried attending mixers in the dorm and had asked one or two women out, but they had turned him down. He thought this might have intensified his upset with Randy and Carol.

In this situation, the discrepancy in psychosexual development of the two friends, who were now roommates, evoked strong and disturbing feelings, to which, fortunately, Tim reacted by seeking help. The themes of exclusion and rejection were apparent. The work of the therapy was to help the student sort out the realistic factors and the underlying family experiences that contributed to his vulnerability and sexual inhibition.

SOMATIC COMPLAINTS

Worry about health and various somatic symptoms can be expressions of larger concerns. General anxiety or obsessional defenses may manifest themselves as hypochondriasis. Occasionally, somatic complaints result from a major physical illness, such as diabetes or asthma, but more often no underlying organic disease exists. When the anxiety relates to chronic illness, the problem may be that the student is failing to observe the recommended medical regimen.

Eating disorders—anorexia and bulimia—appear to be increasing in colleges, particularly among women, and in some colleges represent a frequent presenting complaint (Lee, 1989).

> Constance, a freshman, was referred by the Dean because of binge eating and subsequent vomiting. She was reluctant to seek help, feeling that she was managing successfully on her own. Under pressure she agreed to go for an evaluation. The Dean had become involved because Constance's roommates had become more and more upset by her eating habits and by her vomiting, which they could both hear and smell. They had tried to talk with her directly, but she brushed them aside, saying it was none of their concern. Finally, at the suggestion of the parent of one of the roommates, they took the problem to the Dean, who agreed to speak with Constance.

The sequence of events in this vignette is common. In many instances, students with eating disorders are not self-referred but agree to seek help (which they often feel they do not need) only under pressure from someone else. When the problem is anorexia, the process is further complicated by the fact that the student and the therapist have divergent aims. The student usually wants to lose weight, and the therapist wants the student to gain. Students therefore tend actively to resist referral efforts and, if referral is somehow achieved, to defy attempts at therapy. Whether college authorities have any effective leverage in such situations will vary from campus to campus. Self-help groups for eating disorders on campus are occasionally resources for referral. Although the rules regarding confidentiality apply, it is sometimes helpful and necessary to urge students to involve parents in their care—especially when hospitalization appears likely.

MAKING CHOICES

Making choices may be a problem for a student. This problem can occur in any area in college from choice of courses, to choice of friends, to choice of lifestyle, to choice of extracurricular activities. The following vignette illustrates difficulty over career choice, but, as is usually true if a student comes to therapy with such a presenting problem, issues relating to identity and separation from the family are involved as well.

> Perry, 19 and a junior, sought help for complaints of depression, inability to concentrate, and hopelessness. He wondered whether he should drop out of school. He was a pre-med student making excellent grades, which he thought would delight his father, whom he respected highly. Perry's father was a physician who presumably had always wanted Perry to follow in his footsteps.
>
> Unfortunately, Perry was miserable in pre-med. He knew that he preferred to be a mathematician, but saw no way to do so without disappointing his father. It became apparent in therapy that Perry had avoided making commitments and/or choices in all kinds of important areas of his life having to do with friendships, choice of college, even choice of dress, always in the belief that he might disappoint someone. It appeared that he viewed himself as existing solely for the purpose of bringing happiness to the lives of others, and this happiness was defined in terms of not frustrating others. (There is further discussion of this case in Chapter 6.)

Sometimes a choice that seems rather trivial causes the student more difficulty than might be expected. This happens when the choice touches on deep feelings that are not immediately obvious.

> Stan was a senior who presented with depression in the fall. He had done exceedingly well academically, and in addition had participated in a variety of campus activities. He came to the Southeast from California, having been recruited for his

tennis abilities. While he had made the varsity squad, he had never quite lived up to his advance billing as a player.

His depression appeared to result from his ambivalence about continuing to play varsity tennis. On the one hand, he felt some obligation to the coach and his teammates; on the other hand, he was burdened with considerable academic work and was interested in expanding his extracurricular activities by appearing in a play, which he thought would be fun. His ambivalence intensified until he was in a state close to an obsessional panic and was referred to the mental health service by the athletic team physician.

When choices concern issues of social life, they may include questions about which group to belong to, how to gain acceptance, how to avoid feeling left out of a desirable group, and what kind of behavior to engage in or to tolerate. Sometimes choice at college involves deliberate shifts in behavior as "experiment," or equally broad shifts that seem involuntary and inexplicable. Such changes do not necessarily cause a student to seek therapy, but their consequences may be sufficiently upsetting so that therapy is suggested by someone else.

Jean felt miserable after her first year at college. When she returned home she agreed to see a therapist at the suggestion of her mother. She appeared as a short, slightly heavy, potentially attractive young woman with a disheveled appearance. Her dark, curly hair seemed uncombed and her clothes conveyed an unintended peasant look. She identified herself as an 18-year-old freshman at a prestigious university some distance away, and added that her only sibling, a sister, 21, was supposed to be a senior at the same university but that she had just recently dropped out and gone away with a boyfriend. This turn of events was so distressing to the family that her father said, "Now I have only one daughter." It seemed that this sister, whom Jean loved and admired, had long been a source of concern to everyone.

When the therapist shifted the focus back to Jean, she described a disastrous first year at school. She worried about a rather complete behavior change. A high school merit scholar, she had neglected her college studies right from the beginning and was now facing four "incompletes." A former "social recluse," she had "gone wild" into drugs, drinking, and promiscuity. These activities had culminated in an abortion in the spring. In retrospect, she felt the young man involved had never wanted a serious relationship, and yet she had clung to the attachment, even when, after two months of "fantasy land," he seemed to be pulling away from her. It was at that time that she became pregnant, only to find him sympathetic but not terribly supportive: "He only paid for a quarter of the abortion costs." Jean was quite unable to explain the reason for her irrational behavior and agreed that she needed help. (This case is discussed further in Chapter 6.)

PREGNANCY

Many, if not most, college students are sexually active, and some become pregnant. The pregnancy may be accidental, unconsciously desired, or on occasion, actively sought. The fact of pregnancy has effects beyond the obvious one of creating a new life. Pregnancy confirms one's femininity or masculinity and is also a confirmation of normality, at least in regard to reproductive capacity. It may fulfill an unconscious wish to be both the adult caring for a baby and, through identification, the baby being cared for. It can also express wishes to be close to her mother, or to assert adult independence. Thus, pregnancy can be happy or tragic, wanted or unwanted, intended or unintended, and it is not always easy to determine which, since motivation may be mixed, complex, and, at least in part, unconscious.

In college, separations and losses are important experiences, ranging from separation from parents to broken relationships to shifts of goals and plans. Pregnancy sometimes represents an unconscious wish to replace a loss. The following vignette illustrates the experience of a college senior whose pregnancy appeared to be a response to disappointment, loss, and uncertainty about the future.

Peggy was a senior, intensely motivated, competitive, successful, with a record of outstanding achievement. She was attractive, had had many relationships, and was currently involved with a fellow senior whom she liked but did not love and did not plan to marry. Thus, they were both exploring their own plans for the year after graduation. Her exploration involved a decision to compete for a prestigious prize; this required much effort, including examinations and interviews. Although initially dubious about her chances, she received strong support from faculty, who began to see her as a star who could promote the reputation of their rather small college. She received glowing recommendations, her essay for the competition was very well reviewed, and she made the first two cuts, although she was eliminated in the final round of judging. Understandably, she, her family, and her faculty advisers were disappointed. The latter were nonetheless supportive, and she was awarded another honor, after which life returned to its near normal pace.

Two months later, she realized that she had missed her period, and a subsequent pregnancy test was positive. Since she had always been careful and knowledgeable about contraception, it was difficult to understand how the pregnancy had occurred. Later, she reconstructed the events and realized that, after losing the prize competition, she had felt an emptiness at facing the year she had looked forward to so much. She was grateful to her boyfriend for sticking by her, and she sank into the warmth of the relationship briefly, fantasizing how much simpler it would be not to invest so much in achievement. In retrospect she realized that she had inadvertently miscounted the days of her cycle and had had unprotected intercourse on one occasion. Although consciously she was depressed and upset that she had slipped up and become pregnant, the replacement of the prize by the pregnancy with its life-giving aspects had been an important unconscious motivation.

Students, of course, may become pregnant as a result of ignorance, embarrassment about contraception, or clumsiness. Contraception may also fail because of inexperience, as in the use of a diaphragm, or because of risk-taking, as in using withdrawal as a method. Students may also have a feeling of omnipotence and invulnerability that translates into denial: "It can't happen to me."

For the pregnant student, counseling as to alternatives is important. The controversies about abortion have obscured some of the psychological issues. Although an abortion is not a trivial event, and some women may need assistance with mourning the loss, long-term sequellae are not inevitable. Inherently, abortion does not produce psychological illness, nor long-lasting distress. In fact, the stress and depression may be less than that produced by giving birth and placing the baby for adoption (Koop, 1988). Other women, however, have strong feelings against abortion based on religious or other grounds. Important elements of any counseling procedure include allowing the woman to explore her feelings, to examine as realistically as she can her situation and her alternatives, and ultimately to make up her own mind. No matter what choice is made, it is vital to provide information in as clear and coherent a manner as possible, avoiding a punitive, judgmental attitude.

SUBSTANCE ABUSE

Alcohol and drug abuse may be presenting problems. On occasion, a student will come self-referred; more typically, however, students with such problems will be referred by deans or fellow students because of drunken behavior or drugged appearance. Conduct may range from rowdiness and vandalism to potentially self-destructive behavior such as driving too fast or even suicidal gestures.

> Jack, a senior, was frequently intoxicated, and on one such occasion became involved in a verbal exchange with a Hispanic student. As the interaction became more heated, he called the other student "a damn spic," and this was reported to the Dean. Jack was brought before the Disciplinary Committee, and he was referred for therapy because of his racist remark

and because there was evidence that alcohol was more than an occasional problem. He came to the clinic largely at the insistence of the Disciplinary Committee. He was contrite about his racist remark, but rather consistently denied that he had a problem with alcohol despite considerable contrary evidence and a clear family history of alcoholism.

Jack's presentation illustrates the difficulty of convincing a student that alcohol use, a major component of campus party activity, may be pathological for him, even in the face of clear evidence (Burns et al., 1987; Meilman & Gaylor, 1989).

Similar kinds of presentations may occur with other drugs. A student may assert that getting high on marijuana three nights a week, or even daily, has nothing to do with the fact that he has not turned in assignments on time and that he has missed taking midterms. Hallucinogens go in and out of popularity over time. Some students may use a variety of drugs periodically, some more dangerous than others. This can be attested to by the widely publicized sudden death of a superstar basketball player several years ago following his use of cocaine to celebrate his selection by a professional team. The usual expectation of establishing mutual trust as a given may have to be modified when agreeing to work with a drug-abusing student. Some arrangement for obtaining random urine samples to screen for evidence of drug use may have to be part of the contract in order to proceed with therapy. Regular attendance at Narcotics Anonymous meetings is a useful adjunct.

SEXUAL ASSAULT

Students may come for help because they have been victims of assault. The assailant can be a stranger, on or off campus, but also, more often than has been recognized in the past, the assailant is a man known to the woman student. Date rape and sexual harassment have received much greater publicity recently and, consequently, have generated more concern. It is not clear whether these incidents happen more frequently now than in the past, or whether in recent years women are less likely to feel that they will be blamed and have accordingly been able to talk about such events. Whatever the explanation, they seem to present more often with accounts of rape, often by an acquaintance.

> Lisa, a sophomore, met Grady in the room of a friend. It was not exactly a party, but they each had a beer and discovered a mutual interest in camping and wilderness preservation. Lisa felt that she had finally met someone with similar interests and concerns. It was quite late when the group began to break up, and Grady offered to walk her back to her dorm.
>
> When they arrived, she did not really ask him up, but she didn't protest when he came up the stairs with her. He kissed her good night, but did not make a move to leave, and eventually they ended up in bed with the understanding, Lisa thought, that they might enjoy physical closeness and even sleep together, but would not have intercourse. What Grady understood is less clear in retrospect. In any event, he became more insistent, and using his strength and weight managed to gain penetration. After he left, Lisa became very upset. She felt that she had been assaulted, but was confused because she realized that she had been attracted to Grady and had allowed him to stay over. She came to the health service to try to sort out her feelings and decide whether or not she wanted to press charges—and if she did, what the emotional consequences might be for her.

The account of this event illustrates one not uncommon sequence in which the differing expectations were inadequately communicated, not heard and understood, or ignored. Lisa did not anticipate that her wishes would be disregarded and that force would be involved.

Despite efforts by campus health educators (Yale, 1988), residence hall staffs, and deans of students offices to educate students about responsible behavior, students like Lisa are showing up at student mental health or rape crisis centers. They express feelings of guilt and varying degrees of uncertainty about the rape. Although the student is clear about what she intended to communicate, she may wonder about "hidden signals" she may have transmitted. This is likely to make her feel guilty, even though in reality her refusal to engage in intercourse should be enough and should be respected. In addition to any specific factors idiosyncratic to any such event, such as how well they knew each other, whether either or both had been drinking, even whether they had previously been sexually intimate, a common underlying theme is invariably the man's expectation that "although she said no, she really wanted it." Although much recent literature has stressed that no means no, researchers studying student attitudes about expected sexual behavior have confirmed that many men still believe a woman's no means yes (Ehrhart & Sandler, 1985; Malamuth, 1984; Yegedis, 1986). This attitude changes the meaning of what the man is doing in *his* mind, but it is still experienced as violence and assault by the woman. She will benefit from sensitive counseling, which does not further traumatize or stigmatize her.

VIOLENCE, DEATH, AND SUICIDAL CONCERNS

Incidents of violence and death seem to have been increasing on campuses. These violent happenings include physical assaults, suicide attempts, deaths from accidents, and, rarely, murders. It is unusual on large campuses for a semester to pass without an automobile accident in which at least one student dies. An accident leading to severe injury or even death as a result of intoxication is very upsetting, and, although infrequent, a death from alcohol poisoning is tragic and evokes mourning and guilt.

Suicide is a particularly shocking event that creates great distress on campus. Students who come for help and who express suicidal preoccupation must be taken seriously. An accurate diagnostic assessment and careful evaluation includes obtaining a history of alcohol or drug use, and of prior suicide attempts whether at a time of serious depression or not (Pfeffer, 1988). We have found Schneidman's (1986) criteria assessing the degree of lethality of a possible attempt and the level of perturbation exhibited by the students helpful in deciding whether or not to hospitalize them. In many instances, however, students who kill themselves have not sought help, nor have they broadcast clues about their intentions prior to the event.

In our experience women with personality disorders, or who are survivors of childhood sexual abuse, may threaten suicide or engage in self-injurious behavior such as overdosing, wrist cutting, etc. Many times these students are sent by residence hall counselors, or we learn of them through their roommates or friends who have become overinvolved in caring for and trying to prevent them from harming themselves. In extreme cases, friends will stop attending classes and will restrict personal activities to be with a dysfunctional student who has sworn them to secrecy. A supportive session with the friends or lover can empower these students to extricate themselves from the entanglement and facilitate a successful referral of the disturbing student (Whitaker, 1989).

Any violent event is naturally upsetting to the college community; fellow students tend to identify with the victim, to associate the event with some previous trauma they have experienced, or to feel that perhaps they could have prevented the event. Roommates or friends of the deceased student may come for help. Not infrequently someone from the Student Health Service may be asked to lead a group session or two to help with the mourning process.

> Rachel, a sophomore, was referred for therapy following the alcohol-related death of a fellow sophomore in her dormitory. Although she had not been close to the deceased, she seemed more upset than anyone else in the dorm. The resident advisor tried to talk with her, but Rachel was reluctant to say much. She accepted the suggestion, however, to talk with a therapist.

Rachel was seen for four sessions. She immediately disclosed that the death had brought back vividly the accidental death of her high school boyfriend, who had been killed in a mountain climbing accident a year before. Although Rachel had mourned deeply at the time, and the death at college superficially bore little relation to the death of her boyfriend, the event reactivated some complex feelings that she had about her boyfriend. The opportunity to express some of these feelings to the therapist allowed her to regain emotional control, and after four interviews she discontinued therapy.

Whether this brief therapy dealt adequately with her problem is unclear, but it represented all that she wanted at the time. It is possible that she will return at a later point because it is not uncommon for students to experience "anniversary" reactions in subsequent years, at which time they may relive the traumatic event in fantasy and in their feelings. It is therefore important for the therapist to be aware of such campus events, and alert for possible repercussions.

GENERAL PSYCHIATRIC DISORDERS

In addition to problems more specifically related to late adolescents and young adults who are in college, students may present with any known psychiatric disorder found in this age group. First psychotic episodes with no prior warning may occur on campus. Major affective illness, panic disorders, and obsessive-compulsive disorders are all in evidence. Such syndromes in college students are not significantly different from similar problems in the general population.

4

UNDERSTANDING THE CONTEXT

THE COLLEGE AS BACKGROUND

Colleges are not uniform in their programs, in their rules and regulations, in their expectations of students, or in the extra-academic infrastructure that may determine student social life. Some colleges are primarily residential and expect that the majority of students will live on campus; others cater exclusively to students who commute and offer no campus housing. Some colleges draw students from across the nation; others have primarily a local student body. Some have selective admissions; others have open admissions. Some exist on a large university campus overshadowed by graduate or professional schools; others are separate and may be geographically isolated. Most but not all colleges these days are coeducational. Some colleges encourage part-time students; others have mostly full-time students. Some colleges have strong religious affiliations. Some expect students to graduate in four consecutive years; others have institutionalized methods for students to take time off, or are relatively relaxed about students' enrolling and withdrawing. These differences affect the student's life and influence how the particular processes of learning and maturing will take place; they also affect how closely a student is observed, and how likely it is that problems will be identified and pursued if individuals do not seek help themselves. For example, anorexia and bulimia are more likely to be apparent and to cause concern in residential colleges.

Students, recognizing these differences, usually make an effort to choose institutions that best fit their own perceived wishes, needs, and objectives relating to both educational and personal aspects of college life. If the particular institution is chosen out of necessity rather than true preference, for example, if parental influence has played an inordinate role, or if financial or geographic considerations have been strong determining factors, problems of adjustment are more likely. The smaller the institution or the more specialized or atypical it is, the greater the importance of "fit" or compatibility. When reality deviates from expectations, serious consideration may be given to a transfer, if that is possible. Certain developmental tasks may even be delayed until a more compatible environment has been found.

A therapist working with students should be aware of the college calendar, which will inevitably have direct impact on the student's experience. In addition to the basic calendar dates, such as beginning and end of terms, exam periods, and vacations, there are other requirements that the student must observe, such as deadlines for course choice and course withdrawal, number of courses required to be completed for promotion, decisions about housing, and negotiations about financial arrangements. Furthermore, there may be a series of dates not officially related to the main academic purpose of college but intimately connected to college life. These include athletic events, as a participant or an interested observer, periods for "rushing and pledging" fraternities and sororities, dates for election to extracurricular organizations, and deadlines concerning living arrangements. Certain time periods may increase levels of stress, and the student-patient will probably have expectations of starting and stopping therapy around breaks in the college calendar. These concerns may be novel to therapists who think in terms of major holidays and the traditional August vacation as the only events that warrant interruptions of treatment.

The college community itself represents an environment that may enhance or inhibit the individual student's psychological growth and development. All colleges agree that their major purpose is to provide an academic education for students, either for its own sake or as a step toward graduate or professional education. Colleges are less likely to be explicit as to their role in promoting personal maturity, or in providing help with the maturing process.

Often faculty members respond to students' requests for personal support in an uncertain manner, casting the request in academic terms and stressing either discipline or permissiveness without a clear grasp of either. Even the academic advice may vary widely depending on the individual faculty member consulted, the current campus climate, or the specific institution.

Institutions have different expectations reflecting particular historical periods and also differences in values and style. Some schools emphasize "discipline," others have a more laissez-faire approach. There are periods when faculty recommend originality and "doing one's own thing." On the other hand, students may not be provided with the incentives, guidance, and structures that would allow them to use the freer approach to advantage.

At other times, there is a tightening of discipline and an emphasis on completing requirements. The discipline that is demanded, however, is one that the student may experience as alienating make-work or as an artificial hurdle. Ideally, the student's discovery of discipline in the process of progressive and energetic pursuit of an intellectual task should be an exhilarating experience that no opportunity simply to "get by" can rival. Such discipline is the inevitable precondition of self-discovery and of pleasure stemming from the realization of one's capacity. Ideally, too, teachers and administrators will create and cultivate an environment of balanced freedom and discipline for optimal educational and personal development.

Therapists who work on campus, or who practice in a small community, may be thrust into other situations that inadvertently affect their role as psychotherapists (Grayson, 1986). They may be asked to give an interview for the campus newspaper. On occasion, the on-campus therapist may be approached by college officials and asked to act as a consultant in regard to some perceived campus problem or conflict that is affecting students emotionally. The response requires considerable tact, because almost any public stance that the therapist takes may affect the willingness of some students to seek therapy, especially those that disagree with the therapist's position. Although one can argue that any action that benefits the campus at large is worthwhile, even if it causes a few students to distrust the mental health service, such action is counterproductive if it undermines the image of the service. If this occurs, it may take a long time for trust to be reestablished; thus, the consultant role must be undertaken with great care and sensitivity (Arnstein, 1989; Grayson, 1986).

THE DEVELOPMENTAL TASKS OF LATE ADOLESCENCE

The college years are a period of transition from adolescence to adulthood, and a discussion of this transition may take many forms. Depending on their scientific discipline and training, different theoreticians have described the necessary steps in varying terms. There is, however, general agreement about the tasks to be accomplished. Some feel that these tasks are part of normative development and are independent of culture; others feel that the steps are highly influenced by cultural expectations. Furthermore, in considering the transitional process, one can use various standards as measures. These (Arnstein, 1984) may include a standard of physical or biological development, a standard of intellectual development, a standard of psychological or emotional development, and a sociocultural standard with many variations reflecting different subcultures.

This report is primarily concerned with psychological development, which involves both internal forces and sociocultural forces. The latter affect the course of development and transmit expectations about appropriate social roles for adults in a given society. Sociocultural standards include holding a job, becoming self-supporting, and becoming a parent. These are different for men and women, and among diverse social groups. Neugarten (1971) talks about a "social clock" that is superimposed over "the biological clock." In the United States, her comments about "age expectations of self and others" can be demonstrated by considering educational progress in relation to adult status.

The "normal" age for individuals to finish secondary education is 17 or 18. If they do not go on to college, they may be expected to assume adult social roles rather rapidly. The individual who enters college, however, will usually postpone assuming the full adult social role. This postponement, or psychosocial moratorium, is socially accepted and even considered desirable. Although there are general sociocultural expectations throughout the United States, many subgroups of social class and ethnic background have their own norms, so that there are significant sociocultural differences among students.

It is apparent that the social clock that sets the age when a person is considered to be an adult varies from culture to culture and between different groups within a culture. Moreover, the transition to adulthood is also influenced by the cultural attitudes toward family structure, class stability, and psychological characteristics that are valued by the culture. There are different components to adulthood, such as having a baby and earning a living. An individual's psychological development occurs within its own time frame, however, and social roles that may be assumed at varying times are only meaningful and valid when the necessary psychological development for that role has occurred. For example, a young teenager may become pregnant with a wish to be an adult, and have adult status, with a close relationship to her "own" baby. Yet, if she is very young, say 14 or 15, the psychological development for parenthood has not yet taken place; she has not finished her own adolescent tasks and is rarely prepared to take on fully an adult role.

In the United States, where a considerable degree of individuality and independence is highly valued, particularly in men, the most frequently mentioned psychological task that must be achieved is separation from one's parents. Offer and Offer (1975) state: "The establishment of a self separate from the parents is one of the major tasks of young adulthood. The adolescent must disengage himself from parental domination" (p. 167). Blos (1979) postulates a "second separation-individuation process of adolescence," which he describes as "the shedding of family dependencies, the loosening of infantile object ties in order to become a member of society at large, or simply, of the adult world" (p. 142). Again, by separation, he refers primarily to a psychological separation from internalized representations of parents but does not necessarily include geographic separation from the family. Indeed, for economic reasons increasing numbers of students return home to live with family after leaving or graduating from college. The development of men and women is quite different in this regard. Whether physically close to her parents or geographically separate, independence and individuation for a normal woman is always in the context of important relationships to others (Gilligan, 1982; Miller, 1976).

Erikson (1950) postulated the consolidation of identity, namely, how you see yourself and how others see you, as one of his life crises. Initially, Erikson's (1945) concept of identity related to how a child learns social roles—how he or she is to behave as an adult member of a particular social group. Later, Erikson (1956) expanded the concept to include an internal psychological dimension. Inevitably, the developmen.. of a psychological sense of one's own identity interacts with the need to differentiate oneself from parents. It does not, however, necessarily involve outright rebellion. It is important to remember that values are transmitted from one generation to the next through identification with some aspects of the parents. It is the unique reworking of some values of the parents and other important figures in the past that contribute to the student's own identity, and not simply their wholesale rejection or acceptance.

The development of a capacity for intimate relationships, under which is subsumed the establishment of a satisfactory gender identity and sexual orientation, was designated by Erikson (1950) as "intimacy vs. isolation." He suggested that it is the dominant conflict of the young adult life stage. Here too, women have greater orientation to developing and maintaining intimacy than men (Gilligan, 1982; Miller, 1976). Many theorists feel that the experiences of early childhood provide the crucial basis for a satisfying adult gender identity and sexual orientation. However, the late adolescent-young adult period is a time of considerable sexual experimentation in the search for a true sexual identity (Higgins, 1989), and these experiences as well as those in early childhood influence the person's eventual adult sexual adjustment. Blos (1979) states that the attainment of a stable sense of sexual identity is essential for development. If ambiguity about one's sexual identity prevails, he believes, maturation in all spheres will be hampered.

The late adolescent developmental tasks also include the stabilization of character structure (Blotcky & Looney, 1980; Bryt, 1979; Wittenberg, 1968) and the development of a time perspective (Buhler, 1968; Neugarten, 1969), namely, a feeling for oneself in relation to past, present, and future. Hartmann (1958) discusses the task of adult development in terms of adaptation, which he defines as "primarily a reciprocal relationship between the organism and its environment," and he proposes the concept of "preparedness for average expectable environmental situations and for average expectable internal conflicts" (p. 24).

For many young adults of today, this task may seem more difficult than in past generations. They perceive greater uncertainty about their futures. After years of preparing for a career, positions may not be as readily available as was anticipated. Changing financial conditions, such as inflation, availability of jobs, housing costs, and market swings may affect the ability to repay educational loans and the attainability of expected goals. Changes in roles and opportunities for women within this generation have profoundly affected the way in which young women can use as models the life patterns and experiences of their mothers. In some instances these factors may lead to demoralization. The threat of war and nuclear disaster, while seemingly remote, continues to exist. Thus, it may be more difficult to anticipate average, expectable, predictable trends than in the past.

Friendship is rarely mentioned specifically by developmental theorists; longitudinal studies, however, document the importance of a capacity for friendship for satisfactory later adjustment (Heath, 1979; Katz et al., 1968; Vaillant, 1977). In adolescence, friends are of enormous significance for negotiating the complex process of the move away from home and into the adult world. Friends support, influence, and provide new models, new ideas, and new areas for working out, with a little clearer perspective, issues with parents and siblings. Although gender differences must be considered, changes in friendships may signal important internal developmental changes.

Finally, there is the general need to establish a set of life goals. This need encompasses vocation and anticipated work roles, presumes the capacity for commitment, and requires sufficient confidence and self-esteem to permit the individual to pursue the chosen goals (Bryt, 1979; Buhler, 1968; Lidz, 1968). Hartmann (1960) speaks of this as a *Weltanschauung*, or philosophy of life, and Levinson et al. (1978) speak of a "life dream." This includes the ability to form a personal code of behavior that is acceptable to the individual and that takes into account social norms. For women in the past, social expectations did not lead to the establishment of life goals. Even currently, to do so is problematic, although changing (Heilbrun, 1988).

As previously stated, expectations and developmental paths differ somewhat for females and males (Blos, 1980; GAP, 1975; Gilligan, 1982; Miller, 1976; Ritvo, 1976; Schafer, 1973). Although independence is strongly valued in the culture of the United States, and individuation is an important part of maturation, the value placed on relationships and the impact of the vicissitudes of close relationships, particularly within the family, are usually different for men and women. It is consistent with typical female adolescent development and typical adult female functioning to maintain close ties with family and friends—the kind of attachments that have, in other times, been labeled as dependent. Women tend to maintain these relationships while simultaneously achieving their sense of themselves as individuals, whereas men are less likely to sustain such ties. Individuality and individuation are not synonymous with aloneness. For men, independence can mean more separateness, not only literally, for example, in relation to family ties or friendships, but the self-concept as an independent person who does not need others is more valued and more consistent with a masculine ideal.

Self-esteem in men is often dependent on performance and material success; men are expected to be "aggressive," to be independent and productive, and to compete for high wages and status. Similar competitive aggressive strivings and orientations may take a different form for women. Open female aggressiveness and competitiveness have little cultural support. In addition, the self-concept and ego ideal for a woman often involve her relationships with others, along with ideals of caring, service, and maintaining love and approval. The assessment of separation issues must recognize these potential differences (Gilligan, 1982).

These developmental tasks are involved in many of the characteristic issues that arise in psychotherapy with college students. It is relatively easy to understand their frequent and, in some instances, predictable appearance as themes of therapy. Furthermore, as is so often the case, when an individual enters a new developmental stage, there is a tendency to recapitulate earlier developmental steps. This aspect of the transitional process will be determined by the emotional history of the specific individual and must always be kept in mind. The case vignettes included in this report provide examples of how these themes and conflicts underlie the concerns of college students even when the presenting symptomatology is quite disparate. The therapist working with the college student must be sensitive to the importance of these themes if therapy is to proceed productively.

THE INTERPLAY OF THE COLLEGE ENVIRONMENT AND STUDENT DEVELOPMENT

This section relates developmental tasks to college "milestones." Of course, individuals vary greatly in their development, so any sequential description is imprecise and somewhat misleading. Therefore, the discussion that follows is not to be taken literally as a timetable, or as a lock-step developmental progression for all students on any campus. It is simply one schematic approach to illustrate an integrated way of thinking about the process.

The Freshman Year

The initial event in the college experience is the application procedure and the receipt of acceptance during the spring prior to matriculation. Inevitably the student anticipates the college experience and develops fantasies, either gratifying or fraught with anxiety, or both. Arrival at college almost always begins the process of separation from the family, even if the student is commuting from home, because the college world is much wider than high school, and the college student can be much more independent. Independence, however, can also mean isolation. All sorts of adaptations must occur—academic, social, living—and students are expected to take these steps primarily by themselves, in close association with peers. They must establish their position in a new environment without the accustomed support of home, family, and old friendships, and their self-confidence can be shaken by the presence of many strangers with impressive abilities. It can be a stressful time. A woman student describes freshman anxieties well in this excerpt from her writings:

In high school I finally belonged somewhere. I had established myself as an honor student. I was in the highest classes and was doing fairly well in them. Teachers liked me, and I got away with a lot. Now I have been stripped of all my former security. The place I set for myself is no longer there.

I miss my past. It's not that I don't like this school, or the friends I've made, or anything. For a while I was on the top—good grades, President of the Youth Corp, student director for the school plays, and, most importantly, I was well liked. I had many friends, and was "one of the guys." Even though that started to shatter towards the end, it was basically still there. Now, I am afraid. I am afraid that with all of the new friends we will be making, we will lose contact with each other. I am afraid I will no longer be at the top of anything. I hate the idea of having to start all over again.

College isn't living up to high school. Whereas once I was special-unique, now I am a social security number—one of 10,000 or so numbers. I really don't know what I expect. After all, one only gets out what one puts in. It's times like these, when I'm full of self doubts, that I wonder if life after high school really does exist.

I think that one truly scary thing about college is that it's the beginning of a whole new life. I am no longer under my parents' care. They are not here to help me through everything. I am pretty much on my own here, even though there are many people who are willing to help me. I can't call my parents every day, and ask their opinions, or whatever whenever I want, like before. I have a lot more freedom here, but with that freedom comes responsibility. I'm not sure if I'm ready to handle all of that, yet.

These words, written at the beginning of the freshman year, convey clearly the sense of loss of familiar supports. The task of separation from home might occupy this student in one form or another all through her college years. Even when she feels a less urgent need to turn to her parents for advice and guidance, she will have to come to terms with her "internalized" parents, and struggle to meet or not meet their expectations. Like many students, she may discard some of their values in the process of establishing her independence, and she may even temporarily adopt extreme and adversarial positions.

College really does become the new "home" for students, even for commuting students. College becomes the place where the student forms new associations, explores alternative lifestyles, expands ways of thinking and knowing, and joins new "communities," both on and off campus. Students in residential colleges must learn to live with others in close quarters as assignment of roommates is either random or sometimes deliberately heterogeneous. Roommates or new acquaintances may have different values, some of which may initially seem to a given student immoral or politically outrageous. Yet exposure to these novel ideas may cause the student to wonder about the absolute validity of his or her established beliefs and may lead to a thoughtful reconsideration of values.

Students also confront a range of behavior that may be markedly different from their own, including drinking, using drugs, indiscreet sexual activity, or inconsiderate noisemaking that may interfere with studying or sleep. Learning to cope with such behavior can be a maturing experience, since it helps students think about tolerance, negotiation, and the "rights" of others as well as one's own.

Anne, the oldest child in an upper-middle-class white family, moved from a small, liberal, private high school to a prestigious college. She had traveled and worked in a number of settings as a volunteer, and was a school leader. She was assigned a roommate by computer: a lively, exuberant black girl from the inner city on scholarship, who had "made it" from a tough background. Anne's liberal values prepared her to be accepting and tolerant of differences. They didn't prepare her for the psychological adaptations she had to make to deal with the clash of tastes, colors, foods, music, hours, and friends, nor for the internal conflict that her rising resentment stirred up in the face of her values to be tolerant and accepting. She felt that her reactions were not "justified," yet they prevented her from studying, sleeping, and being comfortable at school.

Students who live in rented rooms or apartments rather than dorms may be faced with chores that have always been done by others at home, or with different standards of privacy and cleanliness. Students vary in their reaction to these challenges. Some retreat to the comforts of a familiar situation by picking friends very much like the peers they had at home. Others may insulate themselves within specific ethnic, religious, or social groups. Some seek out living arrangements that are as similar to their former home as possible, while others become entranced by the new and different peers they have discovered, and rapidly adopt new ways of thinking and behaving. Still others gradually and sometimes cautiously allow themselves to consider and try out the divergent views of roommates and other fellow students.

Experimentation is particularly common in the sexual sphere (GAP, 1965). Despite the current general increase in acceptance of sexual behavior, many students are reluctant to engage in sexual activity and are quite conflicted about relationships. The move toward intimacy can be as threatening as it is comforting, and they may confuse sexual intimacy with personal closeness. Currently, anxiety about AIDS and other sexually transmitted diseases seems to be acting as a deterrent to casual sexual encounters (Keeling, 1989). Discussions about responsible sexual behavior are offered in a variety of settings by campus health educators. Condom dispensing machines are placed in dormitories and bathrooms of public buildings, but celibacy is also promoted as an acceptable choice (Steinfirst et al., 1985).

Within the past two generations changes have occurred on residential college campuses that may put added pressure on students. Colleges no longer see themselves as being in loco parentis. Thus, less mature students who feel a need for "parental" support and structure can no longer rely on institutionalized sources for guidance or the setting of limits. For some students this will be frightening; for others it will be an invitation to adventure.

The first sustained home visit usually occurs at Thanksgiving or Christmas. For students who struggle with prolonged separation problems, the visit is a welcome event, but for others who have enjoyed the freedom from parental oversight, the visit home may be anticipated with considerable ambivalence. The difficulty is increased in those situations where one or both parents have begun to extrude the student from their lives. Students may well feel that there is no place for them at home, or find that their new life at college is of little interest to others in the family. The family may have difficulty accepting the student's pattern established at college of coming and going at will and may expect the student to adhere to family routine. The student's increasing sense of self as a young adult may not be understood at home. To the family, the student seems the same in December as in September, and the family's inability to perceive change may lead to some alienation.

Gradually, the student may become discouraged, feel disillusioned with the parents, and question the validity of the previous idealization of them. Even the old camaraderie with high school friends may appear to have changed, and the student may begin to think about returning to campus and even start counting the days. It is not surprising for students to be aware of sadness, and to experience a range of emotions typical of a mourning process. The commuter student, of course, does not have the sharp break from home and then return at vacation time, but a similar process may occur more gradually until the commuting student finds all sorts of difficulties living at home that had not existed previously.

For some, the often long winter break serves to reconsolidate the ties to home, and it is with reluctance or dread that the student contemplates the return to school, reliving yet again the September separation.

Kim was a lackadaisical teenager who was frankly shocked when she was accepted at a good college at some distance from home. During her first term she made an effort to study and fit in but felt homesick and isolated. She found a friend and counselor in a male graduate student who was the resident advisor in her dorm. She developed a crush on him, and called him several times during the Thanksgiving weekend and again at the winter break, which stretched long into January. It was only through his persuasion that she managed to tear herself from home to return for the second semester.

He encouraged her to see someone at the mental health service. In her first session she described the pull she felt to remain at home. She said the longer break between semesters was much harder for her to end, because it had allowed her to settle comfortably back into the familiar structure of family and community without the anxieties of all the new challenges at school.

The reworking of these issues may suffice to enable the student to be successful during the second semester. For a few, there may be transfers to a school closer to home or a complete return to the perceived safety of the family.

Kevin had been near the top of his high school class academically and faultless in behavior. He was his parents' pride, especially since his older brother had worried them with small teenage delinquencies and had been accepted by only one college the year before. Kevin was accepted in the engineering school of a well-known university, and bade his family good-bye with good spirit and great confidence. The competition at his college proved far more challenging than he had anticipated, however, and he was disappointed that only a couple of students from near home became his friends.

At home for Thanksgiving break he managed to get in trouble with the law for a rather silly prank, but it necessitated his returning home on two occasions for court appearances. At the semester break, he announced to his parents that he had applied for and been accepted at a state university engineering program located not far from home. He justified this move on the rationale that he could excel in this program without the enormous pressure he had been feeling. The counselor he had consulted had listened empathically, had recognized in his illegal behavior a developmental conflict, and in the end had supported the transfer, recognizing Kevin's need to stay closer to his family, to be successful, and to compete with his older brother.

Kevin's difficulties could also be viewed as a response to his family's recurring favorable comparison of him with his brother. At college, away from home, he may have been experimenting with less inhibited behavior and new patterns of thinking, perhaps in order to break the bonds of always being the "good son." During his holiday at home, his illegal prank may have been caused by a breakthrough of repressed impulses resulting from internal pressures to be free of those self-imposed constraints that were necessary if he were to remain his "parents' pride." His delinquent behavior could be seen as an unconsciously motivated statement to his family of his independence and, developmentally, as an important psychological step in trying to find his true self.

The separation-individuation process has the effect of beginning the assimilation of varying aspects of the self into a more consolidated personality organization. Thus, Kevin's decision to return closer to home following upon the illegal behavior can be seen as a regressive attempt to reestablish the repressions that existed in the old family patterns; these at least were familiar, more comfortable, and less consciously disturbing. If this view of the situation were accepted, a therapist would seek to facilitate the developmental process by being less supportive of the apparent precipitous decision to transfer, and would focus on the dynamic issues involved in Kevin's dilemma, while maintaining the usual neutrality regarding the student's decision.

If there are no untoward events, such as a roommate or best friend leaving school or the receipt of poor grades, the second semester (or quarter) starts easily because college is now more familiar. The transition to college as a new (if somewhat temporary) home is completed, and the student may be eager to become more involved with all aspects of campus life. A real commitment to learning may occur. At the same time, the student remembers visits home with a certain undercurrent of sadness, disappointment, loss, and perhaps anger, which, if poorly recognized, may evoke some loneliness and feelings of depression.

A subtle shift in peer relationships often takes place in the second semester. Initially, college relationships may serve as substitutes or replacements for parents or siblings, and are often direct responses to separation anxieties. After the visit home, a different and more meaningful relationship may be sought, an attachment to a person who can respond to what is perceived as one's true self. Relationships may shift to involve more directly the developmental task of consolidating sexual identity. If relationships have progressed in a satisfactory manner, a solidification of sexual identity and some further advance toward a capacity for intimacy may occur. The process, however, may also evoke earlier sexual conflicts and cause the student to seek professional help.

After the first few months of the second semester, many students feel less conscious conflict with their parents, their need to declare separateness is diminished, and they can concentrate on academic tasks and peer relationships. Spring vacation may evoke memories of the Christmas break, but, anticipating just such a reaction, some resourceful students will evade separation problems by minimizing time at home. They will visit friends, or travel with a group of friends.

Following spring vacation, the last weeks of the academic year for many students are characterized by a determination to study and to meet any academic demands that may have been neglected. Simultaneously, there is the realization that the end of the year is approaching, necessitating summer plans and possibly a return home for the summer. For some students this may revive the discomfort of dealing with parents who appear determined—by insensitivity or design—to keep the newly emerging adult as dependent as if still in high school. If a change in the relationship to parents has been achieved and can be sustained, it may prove helpful in coping with a long summer at home.

For most students, the separation issue is taken in stride,

and, after an initial adjustment, it plays a secondary role to other developmental tasks thereafter. For others, the task of separation from home may actually occupy them in one form or another through all four college years.

The Sophomore Year

For the sophomore, the year usually begins more soberly with less anxiety about "making" it. If academic and social success have not already been achieved, what is required is at least more clear. Therefore, a different type of concern emerges. Much of what was undertaken during the freshman year was in response to the advice of parents, teachers at school, or advisers at college. More or less suddenly, students begin to wonder why they made this or that choice and whether the choice was really theirs or someone else's. Who am I? What do I believe in? Where am I going? How do I see myself sexually? Whom do I love? How do I love? What do I want to do with my life? What kind of person do I want to become? These are the basic questions about the core aspects of the self (often referred to collectively as "identity") that come to the fore at this time. The process of answering these questions is usually described initially as "identity reorganization" to be followed by "identity consolidation." The objective is to develop a solid, cohesive identity, which will be felt to be one's own and not imposed by some outside force or person, and which will continue over time. Friends or social groups that were chosen during the freshman year because of propinquity may be reconsidered and new friends sought. Students need to make decisions about extracurricular activities. Thus, the year may be spent considering how to apportion energies for the remainder of college.

For most students, this forward movement in identity formation is punctuated by periodic regressions to earlier patterns of behavior. Usually one thinks of such a return or regression as a retrogressive mechanism associated with pathological conditions; in this instance, however, it is not. Blos (1962), in particular, has advanced the theory that such a shift in adolescence is the only time in the life cycle when regression is a normal part of development. Although others do not agree with him, he feels that it offers the only path to achieve new adult solutions. The nearest approximation to this concept may be the regression that is believed to accompany some creative acts. In adolescence, the individual uses this process to assist in reorganizing old and new components of identity, selecting some to integrate into the personality, and rejecting other components. These processes are both conscious and unconscious.

The first step often occurs toward the end of freshman year. The choices that seemed clear at the beginning of the year no longer seem so "right," and there is a growing uncertainty about a variety of choices to be made. Students worry about whether they are being "themselves" or are products of their parents' expectations. Anxiety may increase, and the student may feel vulnerable to an "identity crisis" (a popular if somewhat imprecise syndrome patterned on Erikson's [1950] concept).

The second step consists of two simultaneous processes. One is the rejection of those parts of the self that are consciously identified as being imposed by others or, for a variety of reasons, are considered undesirable. The other is the assimilation of desirable attitudes that have proven their value by remaining relatively constant over time. These then become intermingled with the newly revived components of the self, which have lain dormant and which are now waiting to emerge into consciousness. This second or reorganizing step is very fluid with active oscillation between some moves back to earlier adaptation and reconstitution of newer ones. It can be a most unstable time for some students, whose conscious experience may involve confusion and anxiety.

The accompanying feelings can be intense, and at times students may question their sanity. On the one hand, it is a relief to be free of old involuntary identity components. On the other, it is also dangerous, because those components provided a stable, even if not completely satisfactory personality base.

Students may alternate from "I feel so confused about myself" to "I feel a new sense of myself." But vicissitudes of the process may be such that, at times, the statement becomes: "I am no one."

Florid symptomatology may appear, which superficially resembles that associated with serious pathology. Not infrequently, mistaken diagnoses are made in late adolescence, especially if one is not aware of the normal psychic fluidity at this time. If the individual is initially fragile, the regression may indeed set off a temporary pathological emotional state that requires immediate treatment to forestall a more serious disorganization. The student may feel isolated and lonely, and a close relationship may be helpful in sustaining the individual through the process.

Sadness is always present. There is mourning for the loss of the old self, the old identity, and the old images of the parents. The loss of the idealized parents at this time is more final and irreversible than ever before. Past accomplishments may be devalued, and future efforts considered useless. An identity crisis of this kind can often lead to a temporary period of indifferent academic performance as well as the state of anomie called "sophomore slump." Although positive experiences can significantly ameliorate the confusion and fragmentation of a severe identity crisis, some of these students will go on to develop borderline personality disorders or other disabling illnesses as adults (Josselson, 1987).

A further step toward identity formation usually occurs toward the end of the sophomore year. The relevant self-statement can be: "I think I am becoming myself!" By this time, the basic components of identity are more or less in place, and the student feels a reasonably coherent wholeness, a sense of self that is basically unique and is for the most part devoid of unwanted or alien aspects. It may be recognized consciously as an internal state of perceived steadiness, a sense of certainty about one's self, and a general feeling of well-being. A psychological "fit" or rightness for that person now exists and, to use

Erikson's (1946) phrase, "the self-sameness and continuity in time," which not only encompasses the experience of the past but also predicts consistency in the future.

As previously noted, most colleges require students to declare a major during the sophomore year, a choice that often relates to future "work identity." Given everything going on psychologically at this time, it is remarkable that anyone ever chooses the "right" major, but it is this very process of identity reorganization that increases the possibility that the choice will be right. Of course, for some students the choice proves to be another "tried on" role, later to be discarded or changed if identity formation is not complete. For others, the need to declare a major serves as an anchor in reality that helps to modulate the extremes of regression and identity shifts.

The choice of major does force the student to consider career choices. If identity consolidation has not occurred, there may be considerable anxiety about the decision. Students may be more aware of what they don't want to do than what they do want to do. These conflicts are often displaced onto academic concerns such as: "I'm getting clearer about what I don't want to study, but what do I want to study? And what do I really want to do and be in life? Is it my fault that I'm feeling disillusioned and that I'm not learning anything—or is this just a lousy school?"

The following vignette describes one student's difficulties in choosing a major and how that decision became entangled in career choice.

> Morgan, now a second semester sophomore, had always been a reasonably good student and had done especially well in science during high school. He was not really interested in science, however, and without much hesitation planned to major in English, but with no real thought of pursuing a related career. If anything, he thought of merchandising, but it was with little enthusiasm or expectation of success. Because of increasing anxiety and concern about these issues, he sought therapy.

During treatment he came to realize that he had eliminated law from his possible career choices because he projected some quality that automatically caused people to ask him whether he was going to law school. In an effort to resist what he felt was a stereotyped response by others to him, he had refused to consider law. As a result of this insight, he reconsidered and thought about applying to law school. However, he found that the issues were more complex. He deferred a decision, and after further soul-searching (and therapy), decided that perhaps his interest really lay more in the scientific field. Ultimately he applied to medical school.

Morgan's experience indicates that identity issues may remain partially open for some time and influence choices, including career, in a complex and tortuous manner.

Contact with parents during the summer following sophomore year helps to further solidify students' identity. Additional role models and nonfamilial life experiences at this time can help give sophomores direction not only to the kind of person they want to be, but also to the kind of life they want to live and the kind of work they may want to do in the future. Sophomore summer may provide an opportunity to explore occupational choices, as well as to earn needed or extra money for school expenses.

The Junior Year

Juniors usually start the year with more realistic expectations and with fewer idealized fantasies. Their better sense of self and especially of sexual identity provides them with a more solid base for romantic relationships. There is a greater readiness to test seriously the depth of an ongoing relationship, or to become involved in a new one with the belief that it can be more committed, loving, and stable. Similarly, juniors approach academic work with a greater commitment and a real desire to explore knowledge in depth. Learning proceeds at a rapid pace, and overall productivity increases remarkably.

Midway through the junior year, students begin to experience a growing sense of their major. Classes are smaller, and students are less anonymous and more willing to take responsibility and to aim for achievement. Students who are disappointed in their major may attempt to change to a more compatible course of study. Parental expectations can have a profound influence on the career aspirations of their children and, either by implication or directly, on the major that they select and the courses that they pursue. If parental influence interferes with the student's own self-determination, and/or if, unbeknownst to both parent and student, unconscious factors are at work, psychotherapeutic intervention may help elucidate and untangle the impasse.

On occasion, the choice of the major may interact with and have an impact on other aspects of the college life experience as well. Consider the following description of a student who moved off campus into a shared apartment in hope of more freedom and increased closeness with friends.

> Carl came to treatment in November of the first semester of his junior year. At the beginning of the semester, he had elected to move out of the dormitory and to take an off-campus apartment with three of his good friends. He came to the mental health service because of chronic resentment toward his three friends and vague feelings of guilt about feeling so angry at them all the time.
>
> During their sophomore year, the four friends had looked forward to having a place of their own so that they could relax, drink beer, have bull sessions all night, and pretty much do as they pleased. Of course, there were very few rules in the dorms against this kind of activity, but some degree of consideration for peers during evening study hours was required, so now they would all escape such "rigidity."
>
> Carl was a pre-med student, and early in the semester he became fascinated by embryology. When he tried to study in the apartment, he was accused by his friends of being unsociable. He stayed in the library for increasing amounts of time, and when he finally did return to the apartment, his

friends were annoyed with him for not socializing with them. He felt angry and resentful, but guilty that he was not being "the sort of person that I had been with them."

Within a few sessions, he decided that his commitment to his studies and to pre-med was sufficiently important to him that he decided to move back into the dorm for the second semester. Fortunately, despite the move, he was able to maintain a good relationship with his three friends.

Intellectual development is obviously one of the goals of college. Such cognitive development consists in acquiring a wide variety of skills, such as writing, critical thinking, original thinking, intellectual productivity, and, for many, a measure of artistic creativity. In recent years, some of the principal stages of that progression have been charted (Perry, 1968). Thinking in college, if all goes well, proceeds from a phase of absolutism, that is, a belief that there is "a right answer," to the capacity to sort out conflicting theories and to develop hypotheses that both better fit old facts and lead to the discovery of new ones. This intellectual development is dependent on many supporting circumstances: the challenge of the right collegiate environment, such as teachers who enjoy teaching, peers who encourage each other to explore rather than to regurgitate facts or do just enough work to get by, and a relative freedom from the effects of conflicts from the student's past.

Intellectual milestones are marked by a further internalization of the motivation to learn, an expansion of curiosity, and an increased capacity to produce. There is, in addition, an emerging ability to become an intellectual coinquirer rather than a recipient who is only vaguely aware of the principles and methods underlying the formulas and statements that have been memorized. Psychological conflict may impede this progression. For example, early in college there may be experiences that revive feelings about previous competition with siblings. Almost every student is confronted with peers who are superior in some areas. This can lead to decreased self-confidence and an angry sense of competition. Students, who have more or less come to terms with their role in the family before entering college, now confront an array of energetic "siblings" all competing for recognition, a competition that is increased by the common practice of grading on a curve. Students may become uncertain about their ability to succeed in chosen careers; this, in turn, can lead to demoralization and the emergence of a host of symptoms that call for therapeutic intervention.

As the college years progress, especially in the junior and senior years, recognizable personality traits, which will form the ultimate character structure of the individual, should crystallize.

The Senior Year

The senior year is a time for consolidation of the newly elaborated and integrated personality as the student prepares for graduation and the realities of the adult world. Two paths are usual: graduate study or a job. If the latter path is chosen, financial independence becomes a realistic possibility and may be the final step toward psychological independence from parents. Is the identity structure sufficiently established to allow a shift from the familiar work of education to a new and very different type of work in the commercial world? Does that new work provide a reasonable likelihood of providing a compatible and gratifying career?

In the process of becoming independent, the newly emerging young adult will have made considerable progress in reorganizing the internal infantile images of parents, and must continue to negotiate a workable adult relationship with parents as they are. For some, however, differentiation comes later, and a few remain inextricably bound to real or presumed parental expectations. For almost all students, the approach of graduation can again intensify anxieties about separation as they contemplate leaving the "home" of college. The following vignette illustrates these anxieties:

Ellen was a 21-year-old senior who entered therapy in her hometown during spring break because of feeling "upset and scared." She complained of having no confidence anymore, of no longer feeling bright or pretty, and of seeming out of sync recently with the Jewish community. With some probing, this general dissatisfaction came down to two specific issues: 1) everybody in her crowd had a plan for after graduation (job, school, something!) while she had nothing ahead of her but to return home feeling a failure and a misfit; 2) all her friends had linked up in pairs or groups for post-college living arrangements. She had no one, although she knew she was well liked, even admired by several friends.

The therapist wondered aloud if her feeling of disconnectedness was perhaps precipitated by the impending separation from college. "I feel so left out," she replied, then poured out a number of stories of feeling on the outside. One example concerned some close friends who began experimenting with drugs. It had been terribly important for her to convince them that they were wrong, although she was not sure she disapproved for any significant reason. "I just wanted them to agree with me. I have to convince people I am right." She also recalled a time when she was dating regularly while three of her close women friends happened not to be seeing anyone—and how uncomfortable this situation made her. At another time her boyfriend became fascinated by a counselor training program, and she again felt peripheral and angry at what she called his "cult." "I guess I'm just bossy," she said. "I want my way, my ideas to prevail." The therapist suggested that her "agree with me" may sometimes really mean "be with me."

The hour was ending when she suddenly remembered that she wanted to ask how one knew if one had PMS. After a brief discussion, she was asked when she had last talked to her gynecologist. She said she had never been to one and added with a chuckle, "My mother in her wisdom didn't believe that was important. In her day, a woman only went when she got married." The therapist did not directly pursue the issue of separation from mother, but told her that a gynecological visit might be a good idea now (she is sexually active) and also a place to ask more about Pre-Menstrual Syndrome.

It was left that she could come back to talk when home

again for the summer following graduation if she still felt upset. A few weeks later, she called in a cheery mood to announce she wouldn't be returning for therapy. She had found a teaching job in the city where she went to college and would be returning there. While she hadn't found a permanent roommate yet, she would be staying with two friends from school until she found an apartment.

For many seniors, the anticipation of a full-time job and earning sufficient money to support themselves is eagerly welcomed. They have successfully negotiated the institutional milestones and the developmental tasks of these years, and they look forward with a sense of pleasure to getting on with their lives. Furthermore, they may anticipate a new level of commitment in a relationship that could be permanent and that could lead to marriage and parenthood.

For others, leaving college reactivates separation issues and questions such as: "Can I leave my friends?" "Can I stop being a student?" "Can we continue this relationship long distance or should we break up now?"

But decisions regarding jobs and/or graduate study must be made. Students may decide on graduate school more to avoid escalating anxiety and true career commitment than to pursue further an area of genuine academic interest.

Jane had enrolled as a graduate student in June and came to the student mental health service at the end of the first term of summer school. She was depressed and anxious and said that she didn't know where she wanted to be, although she was "certainly happy to be enrolled here."

Jane had grown up in an almost symbiotic relationship with her mother and three sisters. She had been next to the youngest and had experienced great loneliness and depression when each of her two older sisters had gone off to college. When it was time for her to attend college, she was admitted to the same college they were attending, and so continued her uninterrupted attachment to them. When each of them finally graduated, Jane succeeded in feeling as if they were "still there" via her close attachment to her peers, some of whom had been her sisters' friends.

When Jane was a senior, it suddenly occurred to her that she was about to graduate and leave all of her friends. She became extremely anxious and went to visit her oldest sister, who was a graduate student in another, not too distant university. While there, she applied for admission to graduate school and was accepted. She returned to her own college for only a few weeks in May, did not say goodbye to anyone, did not attend her graduation, and left to room with her sister until her own graduate studies commenced in June.

Jane's choice to attend graduate school was largely determined by her difficulty in separating from her family, in this instance her sister, and was in no sense a decision about any particular career choice. Her depression resulted in part from the need to focus on a field of study with an intensity she had not experienced in college and with an enthusiasm she did not really feel. Her continuing and basically unresolved career decision and her psychological dependence on family represent an area of vulnerability in her life.

Throughout the academic year seniors are continually oriented toward its end, both in terms of moving on from college and in terms of commencing a new era. This duality is intensified on graduation day when both past and future are eclipsed by the present sensation of having arrived. Psychologically the experience of that moment is determined by the student's internal perception of adulthood and by the answer to the question: "Do I really feel like an adult?"

Seniors who seek treatment frequently realize unconsciously that they cannot answer this question affirmatively, and the attendant anxiety motivates them to resolve the developmental tasks that are becoming increasingly difficult to ignore as graduation looms. The realization that "something is amiss" often begins to surface in the first semester of senior year, usually in the form of symptoms. After more than three years in college with reasonable success in a variety of activities, and with post-graduation plans taking shape, there is an unaccountable feeling of sadness or even a mild depression along with a diffuse sense of incompleteness. Most seniors have accomplished much of the consolidation process and do not have serious residual developmental problems. Although there is the potential for old family patterns to be repeated, there is also the capacity for new patterns to emerge.

By the second semester, seniors may begin to sever their ties to the institution by phasing themselves out of campus activities. Those who have not dealt adequately with post-graduation preparations may have serious difficulties in getting work completed, with the unconscious intent of remaining and not graduating. Those who do not believe that they really have "arrived" feel that they need more time, and they may indulge in similar procrastination. The task in therapy is to make this internal perception more conscious and then to define its components. The knowledge that treatment can help, even if a full resolution cannot be accomplished immediately, is usually enough to reduce their procrastination sufficiently so that they can graduate.

When beginning college, the students' sense of self may not be very firm. They are subject to more or less grave self-doubt and are vulnerable to a host of challenges. Probably nothing is as important during the undergraduate years as the development of healthy self-esteem. It helps students to make choices of occupation, friends, and marital partners based upon a realistic sense of self and capabilities. Students with low self-esteem will passively submit to situations and circumstances; those with high self-esteem will seek to transform them creatively.

We reiterate that the four year sequence presented here is schematic and at best an idealized description. It applies primarily to those students who have had a continuous four years at one institution. Students who interrupt their education or who transfer from one college to another may experience significant variation. Other students are dealing with broader life concerns, such as financial exigency; for them, these issues, while present, may be subordinate.

5

PSYCHIATRIC ASSESSMENT OF COLLEGE STUDENTS

The initial or assessment interview is crucial. Indeed it may be the only session a therapist has with a student; consequently, it must be conducted thoroughly and carefully. Like most adolescents, students are very sensitive to the interest, honesty, and integrity of the therapist. The interview may be their first encounter with a therapist, and the impression they form will affect many things: their willingness to confide, their ability to use the help that is offered, and their inclination to seek treatment later in life if the need arises. Students come for help for many reasons and by various routes. Most are self-referred and arrange a scheduled appointment in advance, some drop in, some arrive in an emergency situation, and some are referred by a medical clinic, by concerned professors, by deans, or are brought in by friends.

Students who are self-referred have a wide range of problems; on average, however, they present less serious pathology than those referred by others. If it becomes clear early in the interview that the problem does not require a dramatic intervention, such as the infrequent need for hospitalization, the therapist and student can clarify the issues and explore the relevant factors that have contributed to the distress. Ideally, this process of exploration and clarification leads gradually to the establishment of an alliance between student-patient and therapist and eventually to an agreement about a therapeutic goal. If the outcome of the assessment is to recommend some psychotherapy, the therapeutic "goal" can act as a "therapeutic contract."

Most college mental health centers and counseling services do not schedule students for an initial screening evaluation. Instead they are seen by the first available therapist who has open time matching the student's schedule. There may be a waiting period that can vary with the academic calendar; generally it is longest during midterm and final examinations and toward the end of the academic year. These represent the periods of greatest demand for consultation/therapy. Some centers arrange for peer counseling (D'Andrea, 1987; Salovey & D'Andrea, 1984), extra walk-in hours, or cut back on regular therapy hours in an attempt to meet this demand. Other centers are organized to provide an initial evaluation interview with minimal wait followed by assignment for therapy if that is deemed desirable. If no therapy time is open, the student is placed on a waiting list which is managed so that more urgent cases may receive priority.

Some clinics attempt to maximize the efficiency of the first interview by having the student fill out a questionnaire which requests demographic data and the student's reasons for seeking consultation. The therapist can review this data and, in a health center, also scan the student's medical record before beginning the interview. Thus, the therapist may discover conditions that could easily be missed or misdiagnosed, such as medical illnesses that are accompanied by psychiatric symptoms, or administrative problems that concern the student. After some preliminary general exploration, the therapist can focus directly on these identified issues. Of course, some students may resent filling out such forms, considering them impersonal; such students would prefer to come in and "just talk," and they should be allowed to do so. The questionnaire can be helpful, however, to highlight major psychiatric or medical concerns and complications.

Therapists have a large agenda for the first interview. They want to know why the student seeks help, what the student thinks the problem is, and what the student expects from the encounter. Why the student comes at this particular time is of special importance. The therapist tries to determine whether the student's stated problem is the real issue or a displacement, the extent and seriousness of the problem, its effect on the student's life and functioning, and the factors that increase or decrease the student's ability to cope with the problem. At times, students may give a somewhat confused account of their concerns. Particular attention is then devoted to clarifying and eliciting the major complaint, and to assessing what type of therapy may be useful to the student. As the student talks, these concerns are present in the therapist's mind and influence the conduct of the interview.

The interaction between student and therapist is complex and occurs on both conscious and unconscious levels. The therapist integrates direct observations with clinical judgment, formulates tentative hypotheses, and then tests these formulations by probing gently to see whether they apply. Moreover, the therapist's formulation of the nature of the student's problems is usually fluid, not very explicit, and may be based largely on empathic understanding, using knowledge of people, of psychiatric theory, of psychodynamic concepts, and of culture and behavior. The flow of information is facilitated by establishing an atmosphere of respect and interest, which permits the student to express feelings and thoughts with minimal danger of being judged, criticized, or rejected by the therapist. In such a setting it is possible for students to confide thoughts and concerns that have bothered them, but that they have been reluctant to express to friends or family.

Therapists are usually trained to focus on their own feelings as guides to patients' difficulties. Consequently, how a therapist feels during an interview may be one of the best indications about the nature of the student's problems. For example, a therapist frequently experiences a responsive feeling of sadness before consciously noting the patient's sad face, hunched posture, low voice, slow speech, and a complaint of lack of energy that add up to a diagnosis of depression.

The form of the interview is generally open, as students tend to be verbal, self-absorbed, and interested in knowing more about themselves. In a supportive atmosphere, they are often able on their own to make the connections between their distress, possible etiologic factors, and options for resolution. The therapist may facilitate the process through subtle direction by showing interest in certain subjects, ignoring others, and attempting to clarify ambiguous or vague, but emotionally laden statements. When the therapist discerns a connection between two seemingly unrelated events, or between past and present occurrences in the life of the student, a tentative interpretation may be made. In this way, the therapist may try to engage the student and demonstrate the process of therapy during the assessment phase. In other instances, the therapist may simply be supportive and reassuring and act primarily in an educative capacity.

As the interview progresses, the manner in which a student presents complaints and relates to the therapist influences the course of the process. It is essential to adopt an active form of listening and to provide feedback to the student. For example, if a student appears insecure, the therapist may attempt to be overtly supportive and encouraging; if a student is over-enthusiastic and verbose, the therapist may try to focus the discussion; if the student's account is confused, the therapist may ask clarifying questions; and, if the student is suspicious, the therapist may recognize that more time or a second interview is needed to try to establish trust. While these various responses to the student's perceived difficulties can be helpful, the therapist must also try to inquire about and understand the meaning of the observed behavior.

It is important to obtain the student's relevant past and family history, but only *after* the presenting problem and current life situation have been explored in some detail. For many students, separation-individuation impulses make them reluctant to focus on past and family history. When this background information is obtained, however, the therapist gains insight into the student's expectations in terms of upbringing, culture, and familial behavior; learns about the stresses in the student's past, and how they were handled; and obtains some sense of the quality of the student's interpersonal life, level of functioning, social support system and degree of psychopathology. Sometimes, in the process of clarifying historical data, the student may have the experience of suddenly understanding the problem, and can even see a way of coping with it. On other occasions, the therapist may summarize and synthesize information presented and open up possible avenues for resolution.

During the process of exploration, it is often possible to determine whether the presenting problem is new, recurrent, representative of ongoing psychopathology, a manifestation of a specific crisis, a result of failure to resolve a developmental task, or a combination of factors. For example, a student may develop severe symptoms in situations that foster the development of autonomy in making choices. By clarifying this with the student, the therapist helps the student appreciate the conflicts associated with the developmental problems, rather than focusing only on the symptoms, and facilitates dealing with the underlying issues. This can alleviate the student's fears about the severity of the problem and help to place the problem in a broader and more useful context. In such situations, the student may not require any further help at that time.

On the other hand, for some students the presenting symptoms are indicative of major psychiatric pathology, which needs to be recognized and dealt with promptly. The following vignette briefly describes the assessment and decisions for subsequent treatment of a more seriously disturbed student.

Noah was a sophomore in a major Southern university who fled home in a panic state at the beginning of his second year. He found that he could not think clearly, had racing thoughts, was constantly preoccupied with sex, could not sleep at night, and was hyperactive. He presented himself for assessment, announcing that he was an "obsessive compulsive neurotic." From age 14 to 16 he had had intensive psychotherapy because of intrusive obsessive thoughts of a sexual nature that interfered with his academic and social life in high school. The assessment revealed a family history of alcoholism, depression, and an uncle who had clearly had several manic episodes. With this history and the mental status exam performed during the interview, it was clear that he suffered from major affective disorder, and was manic. He was promptly placed on Lithium and within a week he became more euthymic. He claimed, "For the first time since I was 14 years old I am able to think straight."

Although clinically much improved, he continued to come for weekly psychotherapy sessions to understand the many prolonged attachments he had retained to his parents, by virtue of his chronic affective illness. He first tried to loosen some of these ties by becoming furious with his family but gradually was able to take distance and to differentiate from them in a more reasonable, less frenetic way. He took the medication as prescribed, moved into an apartment, and transferred to a local college. He established a relationship with a woman, with whom he became sexually intimate, and for the first time was able to sustain a loving, close heterosexual relationship without intrusive obsessive thoughts. He lived on his own in an apartment with his girlfriend, working part-time, and did well academically, finishing his junior year.

Sessions were spaced out as the year progressed, and eventually he and the therapist agreed to stop regular visits, although he continued to come in every few months to have his Lithium level monitored and to "chat" about girlfriend and family issues, which were age appropriate for his year in college. Noah stated very clearly that he did not see the point of more intensive psychotherapy because he felt that he was on his own for the first time in his life, and the therapist respected this feeling.

This student was struggling simultaneously with a serious underlying disorder and developmental issues. His distress was sufficient to disrupt his college progress, but he saw the need for psychiatric help, and the prompt prescription of appropriate medication rapidly led to a reduction of symptoms. He may continue to do well, graduate, and move into the next phase of his life, or may again require more intensive care if his clinical condition deteriorates. The assessment task involved recognizing and providing treatment for the major psychiatric illness first and then more gradually helping him to deal with developmental issues. His developmentally appropriate wish to be on his own was then respected by the therapist agreeing to suspend ongoing psychotherapy.

As described in the preceding case, it is crucial that psychosis, confusional states and dissociative disorders, hypomania, and severe depression not be overlooked. Such severe difficulties can sometimes be discerned early in the interview when a student displays inappropriate moods, unusual or bizarre ideation, hallucinations, delusions, rigidity, twitching, excessive psychomotor activity, abrupt changes in speech patterns, or shifts in the level of engagement. Inquiry about biological functions such as changes in sleep patterns, appetite, weight, or libido are important. These may not only indicate severe disturbance but may be useful guides to the course of the illness.

In general, the therapist may inquire directly about issues of concern that have not come up spontaneously and assess whether any serious danger exists. In cases of severe depression, for example, it is essential to ask about suicidal impulses and plans. The presence of a detailed suicide plan usually indicates serious intent. The danger of suicide is compounded if the student's personal relationships are meager, distant, or troubled. A nonphysician therapist who interviews such a student should refer to a psychiatrist or to a psychiatric emergency room in a hospital to facilitate hospital admission—voluntary or involuntary—if such is indicated, or to consider use of medication as a part of the treatment.

Direct inquiry about drug or alcohol abuse is important, since students are sensitive in these areas and are often reluctant to volunteer information for fear of disapproval or even punitive reaction. In some cases, it will be important to learn specifically about the student's sexual development and sexual life, as well as a broader picture of friends and social support system. A formal mental status examination is usually not indicated unless there is suspicion of an organic brain syndrome or psychosis.

It is important to conclude the assessment interview with a

summary or a clear statement of mutual agreement between therapist and student. This may take the form of a referral, a selection of a focus for short-term therapy, or simply an agreement to meet the following week to continue with the assessment. If it appears that the student has circumscribed symptoms, such as examination anxiety, fear of speaking in public, difficulty in assertiveness, or excessive shyness, a referral to specific behavioral groups or workshops, if available, may be appropriate. Career planning or academic problems call for cooperation with the respective campus agencies or administrative personnel.

At times the initial interview is sufficient to resolve the presenting problem. In other instances a few sessions are required.

On occasion it becomes clear during the assessment the duration of therapy indicated will be longer than that usually provided by a student mental health service on campus. In such instances an important task of the assessment is to identify the probable need for longer term therapy, and to discuss issues relating to referral (Medalie, 1987).

The student will be more likely to accept and follow through on a referral for additional psychotherapeutic work or on other treatment recommendations when the student has collaborated with the therapist in arriving at an understanding about the nature of the problem. Among the issues to consider are the therapeutic opportunities within range of the college and the possibility of obtaining financial support from parents.

It is not possible here to list all the many clinical situations that might require long-term therapy, but any symptomatology or personality problems that have existed over a considerable time period without change might qualify. Most often long-term therapy is not necessary at this time. College students tend to avoid lengthy therapeutic involvement; developmentally they are bent on achieving autonomy and are threatened by situations that foster prolonged dependence, whether on therapists or other adults. Consequently their strivings for independence should be respected, and therapy should be offered that is tailored to their needs and developmental level.

6

ASPECTS OF TREATMENT
WITH COLLEGE STUDENTS

When college students seek psychotherapy for personal conflicts, the therapist attempts to keep an open mind about the advisability of treatment, its type, and duration. Therapists must be ready to address the presenting issues quickly, to get the student engaged in therapy from the outset, to confront the presenting problem or crisis directly, to deal actively with the emotional interplay between the student and therapist, and to be open to consider termination. Therapy may be brief if students receive, or feel they receive, what they need in a few sessions. Duration of therapy may be limited by the academic calendar, or a specific maximum number of visits may be set by the health service to better provide for other students.

It is important for the therapist to engage the patient by showing interest, by listening actively, and by trying to understand what the student is attempting to convey. The therapist must prove to be both trustworthy and capable of being helpful. Students are often wary of counseling or therapy for a variety of personal and cultural reasons. Even an accurate and potentially helpful comment by the therapist may be resisted. It can suggest change and, as such, represent a challenge to the student's self-image and sense of competence; or, it may be heard as a criticism or resented because the student is competitive with the therapist and does not wish to recognize that the therapist may be right.

An important element in psychotherapy is transference. This concept refers to the re-creation in the relationship between therapist and patient of certain significant thoughts, feelings, and reactions that the patient had experienced originally in much earlier relationships, such as with close family members during childhood. Transference involves experiencing these feelings again in the close relationship with the therapist. For example, a student may experience the therapist as a punitive father, always critical and angry, or as a helpful older brother, or as a mother reluctant to allow independent action by the student. The student may feel this way toward the therapist regardless of the way the therapist behaves or the gender of the therapist. Slight similarities between the therapist and significant people in the student's life, as well as the social status, gender, and racial characteristics of therapist and student may have important effects on the manner in which the therapist is perceived and heard, as may the student's past experiences, if any, of being in therapy. In addition, the student often endows the therapist with authority, power, and feelings that the student associates with the college itself.

Needless to say, transference feelings are not the only element that determines the relationship between student and therapist; accurate assessments and responses to the therapist and student as they actually are also play a role. The principles of therapeutic action in psychodynamic psychotherapy, however, recognize the importance of the transference as a vehicle to bring into conscious awareness feelings, responses, and patterns of behavior that may have had their origin years before in important family relationships. Difficulties in the present can be understood and worked with in this context, and more appropriate coping mechanisms can be developed.

The therapist and student form an alliance to work toward the goal of self-understanding as a means of relieving the student's distress and symptoms. However, symptoms may also resolve as a consequence of the therapeutic relationship itself without overt attainment of insight, or they may diminish as a result of suggestions enhanced by the authority of the therapist's position.

As most college students are in late adolescence, the nature of the therapeutic alliance is strongly influenced by the student's perception and experience of the therapist as a parental figure. Inevitably, the wish to separate from parents colors the therapeutic alliance, and the student can use the therapist to aid in the struggle to achieve separation and individuation. This can occur not only in terms of the current relationship with parents, but also in terms of the relationship based on internal images that are residuals of past experiences.

> Perry, the junior (page 28) had felt conflicted about his plan to follow in the footsteps of his highly admired father and study medicine. He was miserable in pre-med and preferred mathematics. Early in the therapy, the therapist pointed out that Perry seemed to feel that he existed only to please others, and that this effort was played out as attempts not to frustrate others, specifically his father. He was able to see that this life goal was impossible, and at the same time began to notice that his father was really rather unhappy being a physician, and that this unhappiness was something that he, Perry, could not resolve.
>
> With this somewhat more realistic view of himself and his father, Perry was able to announce not only to his father but also to his mother that he didn't want to go to medical school. His father responded that this decision was fine, because if he had it to do over again, he certainly wouldn't become a doctor with all of the red tape that doctors have to put up with these days! Perry was greatly relieved, but as the last session was ending, he became convinced that the therapist was "looking unhappy, probably because you think that I would make a damn fine doctor if only I put my mind to it." The therapist replied, "Do you expect me to feel as you had expected your father to feel?" Identifying this as a manifestation of the transference within treatment was helpful to the student in more fully consolidating gains.

While the therapist actively supported separation in this brief treatment, the patient's tendency to see the therapist in parental terms is illustrated by his remark about the therapist "looking unhappy."

A student may also wish to become attached to the therapist, but simultaneously may feel anxious and resist such attachment because it evokes feelings of child-like dependency, especially if the student is offered open-ended, long-term psychotherapy. Thus, a student may become rebellious and resistant in therapy in order to ward off the student's own wish for a return to a closer, more dependent relationship with parents. The therapist may be misperceived as fostering dependency as a condition for providing help. In this instance, the wish for closeness is projected onto the therapist, who then is experienced as dangerous. Thus, the reluctance to become involved in psychotherapy may be adaptive and represent a healthy striving for autonomy, which the therapist may need to support and strengthen.

> Linda (page 25) had come to therapy because of confusion over her sexual relationship with Bob, which had developed despite an emotional commitment to Joe. In the first two sessions, she talked about how this had evolved. She began her third session by reflecting that she had been thinking about the questions raised in the first two sessions. Bob and she decided that it really didn't make any sense for them to be having intercourse. She told Bob that there was no reason why they could not be good friends and fellow workers without having the relationship sexualized. He agreed, and they stopped the sexual encounters. With this change she felt greatly relieved and no longer in need of treatment. The therapist questioned whether she might continue to consider how her relationship with Joe was going. This question was raised because, while she had also been having intercourse with Joe, there was no clarity as to her success in achieving some degree of intimacy with him. However, Linda was not interested in pursuing this, and said she would return if she felt the need.

This exemplifies a situation in which the therapist felt that more therapy might be indicated in order to help the patient better understand what had motivated her to become sexually involved with Bob. However, the student opted for autonomy, and, by not strongly opposing the termination, the therapist encouraged this step.

In working with adults, silence on the part of the therapist promotes development of the patient's fantasies about the therapist and allows the transference to evolve fully. In therapy with a college student, however, silence can be alarming and anxiety provoking, because it may promote a return to less adaptive ways of responding at a time when the student needs help in dealing with the immediate life situation. Listening is an active process; there are many ways to ask about and explore what the student tries to convey. The therapist may repeat or summarize what has been said, with the aim of learning whether it coincides with what the student had in mind. A trial tentative formulation often enhances the process, further engages the student, leads to a therapeutic alliance, and sets a specific task for the therapy. Minimizing a problem or assuring the student that "everything will be all right" is not appropriate, especially when the student perceives the problem to be insoluble and overwhelming. Since the issue is often what events mean to the student rather than the objective reality, the student may feel misunderstood or not taken seriously.

Because the student is in a phase of rapid psychological growth, relatively brief therapy may accomplish more than one might anticipate. Student-patients who raise the question of stopping therapy are not necessarily displaying "resistance" to treatment, or a "flight into health." An ending of therapy may represent an accurate assessment of the student's immediate need; this may be for an independent opportunity to integrate new life experiences and achievements rather than to engage in exploratory therapy.

This is illustrated by the case of Terri (page 23), a freshman who came in distress over her relationship with her roommate.

> In the second hour, Terri revealed a new piece of information, which was probably the trigger for her episode of anxiety and which, in turn, had led her to seek help. She had

"learned" in recent weeks that her brother and only sibling, who at 28 had been a repeated source of disappointment to her parents, was homosexual. This revelation had had a tremendous impact on the family, but, curiously, she felt she had somehow known, because he had "always been that way," although it was never acknowledged or spoken of. Now that it was out in the open, Terri, already struggling with sexual identity issues on an all-female campus, was deeply concerned about her own orientation.

Her great concern was that she would disappoint her parents, to whom she felt a strong, "perhaps too strong," attachment. She was asked to say more about this attachment. She began to try to understand some of what was disturbing her in terms of what she described as her "Little House on the Prairie" upbringing. She had grown up in an extremely sheltered middle-class environment, overly protected by her parents, and largely deprived, she felt, of learning experiences with other young people. She had felt unprepared, except academically, for college life, even in a small women's school. "It was like stepping from a dream world into reality." The therapist suggested that this sounded similar to the harsh experience she had suffered recently when her roommate had started dating and spending less time with her. She replied with feeling that she should not have to lose what was rightfully hers. The therapist replied that they could talk again about what was truly hers, and suggested she might think about that in the week ahead.

In the third session, Terri seemed much calmer. She spoke of her roommate briefly and with a kind of irritation, which differed from the fierce anger she had previously shown. Then, with some glee, she announced she had accepted a blind date for herself and was looking forward to the next weekend. He was a law student, and she thought that he might be interesting since she planned to go to law school after graduation. Furthermore, she would be double-dating with another woman down the hall, who had always been friendly but to whom Terri had paid little attention while she was so absorbed in the relationship with her roommate. Generally, she reported feeling better. There had been no outbursts in the past week. Her dorm resident adviser had spent a lot of time with her, and her parents were coming to visit in a few weeks. She wasn't sure she could find time for them because of a big paper soon due. Because of the paper, she said she wouldn't be making another appointment but asked for permission to call if she felt the need. The therapist agreed and wished her well on both paper and date, adding that some day she might wish to explore further and in more depth some of the issues that had been touched upon.

The student did not call and there was no follow-up, but the vignette illustrates several important points. The brief therapy had centered around the current crises in her life, yet through them, she had gained some insight into her fears about separation. In addition, the "assignment" to think about herself may have been useful in promoting a sense of individuation.

The last session was clearly focused more on her own interests and goals. This young woman had rather significant pathology, as indicated by her occasional poor judgment and poor impulse control, as well as her capacity for libidinal and aggressive acting out, but this brief therapy concentrated on the primary developmental problem in an effort to aid her to return to college. Further therapy was mentioned to encourage her to seek help in the future, and with the hope that she would be more likely to do so if she experienced this first brief encounter with therapy as useful. It also should be noted that the therapist gave her direct support in the final session.

A particular transference problem reflecting directly on developmental issues already described commonly arises with psychologically naive students. These students may come from a background in which it is assumed that one sees a therapist "only if you are crazy." This idea may be reinforced by an attitude that seeking help is an admission of weakness, and that it is really important to "do it oneself." For these students, engaging in psychotherapy undermines a value set and self-image that emphasizes independence and self-confidence, no matter what the emotional confusion or distress. Early in the college experience, when one is comparing oneself with others who seem more competent, the idea of confiding in someone may seem particularly threatening. The value placed on being independent or "pulling oneself up by the boot straps," which is part of the American ethic of independence, may interfere with getting help. Feelings of weakness at the idea of seeking help can also represent the student's striving for independence on the one hand and the wish to be taken care of on the other hand. If the therapist feels that this is an important issue for the student, it should be discussed openly. Otherwise, it is likely that the student will flee therapy and be reluctant to come back when a new problem arises.

Countertransference issues involving the therapist's feelings are important as well. Often therapists are influenced by their distance from their own college experience. Younger therapists are likely to feel close to the college years, leaving them vulnerable to overly identifying with the student; older therapists may feel alienated from current campus culture and unconsciously react in a manner appropriate to their own college days but inappropriate to the contemporary scene. Moreover, for older therapists, countertransference problems may arise when the therapist responds to the student as one would to one's own child. Certain issues, such as choice of sexual partner, drug use, and apparently deviant or self-defeating behavior, may be especially difficult to treat appropriately if these behaviors arouse anxiety in the therapist because they arose or are likely to arise with the therapist's children in similar life phases.

Although it is generally agreed that it is better to be healthy than sick, it is less easy to agree on a definition. Moreover, in this realm it is easy to confuse value judgments with universal truths. Thus, one expert (or culture) may consider independence a component of mental health, while another believes that a more dependent adaptation is preferable. The therapist may believe that maintaining the student in college is of paramount importance, or may be inclined to direct the student toward specific achievement or a profession, rather than helping students explore their own feelings and conflicts about such goals. Thus, in a countertransference sense, the therapist may unconsciously be echoing a parental stance and, consequently, may inhibit the student's exploration and arrival at the student's own decision in contrast to accepting the therapist's/parent's authority.

Another source of countertransference difficulty may derive from idealization of the therapist by the student. It can be seductive and narcissistically gratifying for the therapist to be seen as "a role model." This may compromise the therapist's objectivity as well as subtly dissuade the student from expressing negative feelings toward the therapist. Conversely, the therapist may be reluctant to make therapeutic interventions that challenge the student's idealized view of the therapist. For example, the therapist may be concerned about protecting the patient's idealization of the therapist and, thus, be reluctant to introduce uncomfortable topics that need to be addressed in the therapy.

A particular countertransference problem involving issues of confidentiality and role conflict especially affects therapists who see students in college mental health centers and who are also part of the college faculty or staff. College students are acutely concerned with issues of confidentiality, and students who consult the service must be assured that their confidentiality will be protected. Nothing can more quickly destroy the credibility of any mental health professional an entire college mental health service than a breach of confidentiality that becomes known to students. This includes both the students who are referred by administrators or faculty members because of emotional problems and those who come self-referred. The faculty member is not owed a follow-up report on the student, and none should be given unless there is a specific understanding prior to the first interview that such a report is in order. On the other hand, it may be helpful, with the student's permission, to notify the faculty member that the student has kept an initial appointment. If the faculty member asks what transpired during the visit, rather than divulge information about the student, the therapist should encourage the faculty member to ask the student directly. The therapist can discuss reasons for and the importance of maintaining confidentiality.

Occasionally a student is referred because of disruptive behavior that threatens the institution or other students. Under such circumstances, a member of the college administration or the faculty will make a specific request for an evaluation. In these circumstances a report is usually required and confidentiality is explicitly not assured. The student should be informed of this at the *outset* of such an assessment. This is a rather special case and some services may be unwilling to serve such a function because of conflict of interest. Others are willing to do so in clearly defined situations.

Mental health professionals assessing students in an off-campus setting need to be as aware of these guidelines regarding confidentiality as on-campus professionals, for a breach will immediately undermine any therapy that is contemplated. The following case illustrates some dilemmas related to confidentiality.

> Marilyn, a junior, sought therapy because of difficulty with peer relationships. She was also a member of a women's varsity athletic team. She mentioned in passing her rage at the male coach of this team, who sought sexual favors from team members and rewarded those who complied by advancing them on the team or by allowing them to go on trips to play other college teams. She had not confronted the coach nor informed the authorities about this, nor had the other women on the team. After revealing this, she dropped the matter and went on to other subjects in the therapy.

This case raises questions as to the therapist's responsibility when such information is revealed. Should the therapist take some action? Does the therapist have a responsibility to protect others in the community who may be harrassed? Whatever the answers to these questions, the immediate therapeutic issue hinges on the student's motivation in introducing the sexual harrassment issue. Was it to test the therapist or simply as background to her other problems? Was it to see whether the therapist would take action? Students frequently are adept at inviting this kind of countertransference rescue fantasy, and it is important for the therapist to be aware of this and not be inadvertently seduced by the invitation. It might, however, be appropriate to explore the obstacles that the patient saw to correcting a situation about which she appeared to feel strongly.

When a patient reveals information about harmful behavior by a third person, the therapist may be confronted with a complex set of options. Some behaviors, such as sexual abuse of children, by law must be reported through prescribed channels. Otherwise, in the course of treatment, one does not breach confidentiality unilaterally except in the most unusual circumstances involving a conviction that the patient is sufficiently likely to do harm to self or others. Then, every effort must be made to intervene. Marilyn's situation obviously does not fall into these categories, but rather involves the balance of the student's interests against the interests of the community. In this instance the therapist may feel an understandable impulse to correct a situation that is clearly inappropriate and that may be harming other students. This impulse must be weighed against the effect any action may have on the individual therapy. The therapist must consider whether and how best to help the community without negatively affecting either the therapy for the individual or the reputation of the health service. The therapist who is on campus is in a different position than an off-campus practitioner, who may be less tempted to get involved in issues that are administrative or community-related.

Throughout the report, we have emphasized how brief interventions can have a significant impact on a college student's ability to return to a more effective level of functioning and a greater sense of well-being. A number of models for brief or time-limited therapies have been advocated and described by some theorists and practitioners (Davanloo, 1978; Malan, 1976; Mann, 1973; Sifneos, 1979). Although these models have been successful in certain contexts, when rigidly followed none of these apply to work with college students. Rather, it is the experience of our committee that students come to a psychotherapist for a variety of reasons, and it is preferable to offer an individualized treatment plan based on a careful assessment and a mutual understanding of the student's problems, needs, and expectations (Ursano & Hales, 1986). This position is in agreement with the findings of Strupp's research group at Vanderbilt University (Binder et al., 1987). This might be a few sessions or a more extended psychotherapy. Some students come to experience psychotherapy for the first time, and the goal may be to prepare them for longer term therapy (Medalie, 1987).

In order to give a fuller acount of therapy, two more detailed case examples of relatively brief, but more exploratory types of therapy follow.

Jean (page 29) had sought therapy at the suggestion of her mother during the summer following a miserable freshman year at a college some distance from home. Her sister also attended the college but, much to the family's distress, was planning to withdraw to be with her boyfriend. In the first interview, Jean described a disastrous freshman year in which she went from being a "social recluse" to being quite "wild," ending with an abortion in the spring. She was unable to explain her changed behavior. Jean's boyfriend, she noted, was not acceptable to the parents, but her mother was most interested in Jean's experience with him. "How did it feel?" was her first inquiry. This reminded the patient that, while she had indeed been shy to the point of being socially backward in adolescence, she had lost her virginity to a neighbor boy at 14. At that time, too, her mother had seemed fascinated: "Did you like it?" Jean contrasted her own compulsion to tell the truth about all things with her sister's deceitfulness and secrecy, which hurt her mother. She seemed oblivious to mother's vicarious gratification in their discussions.

Jean had long understood that her sister's rebellious behavior earned only father's anger and mother's distress, "so I saw no one, wrote dark poetry, and got lots of approval at home." Nevertheless, it was clear that Jean in many ways had followed the more adventurous sister: to the same nursery school, grade school, then private girls school, taking the same senior year program in a local college, then on to the same residential college. When her sister took up an instrument, a typing or art course, Jean was quick to do the same. The therapist wondered if Jean felt she had ever chosen something freely for herself, since she seemed to have chosen to do *only* that which her sister had chosen before her. Despite her own recital Jean showed surprise at this observation.

Somewhat later in the hour the therapist pointed out that it seemed Jean cared about her sister, and admired her efforts to separate from the family, but that she herself seemed to be conflicted, to have more mixed feelings, wanting also to please and stay close to her parents. Jean then recalled the excitement she felt about going away to college, the great anticipation of being away from the family. What happened, though, was that big sister set the pace, drawing the patient into her "fast" and older crowd. "I followed her lead," she said, "into pot, sex, parties." She avoided studies and her own freshman peers, but she still got no flak at home. "I'm the good girl," she said.

At this juncture, Jean came to an insight. Her abortion had come about just after her sister's announcement that she was dropping out of school with her male friend. A follower again! "She gives me flexibility," commented Jean. When asked if there was some price to pay for this, she began to talk about the interplay within the family. "I end up picking up the pieces after her." She described frequent, endless conversations at home, focusing on her sister's wayward behavior, but pulling Jean into an awkward position. She felt she had to reveal, but did not want to betray; she wanted to help her sister, but realized she was resented for being in the parents' favor. She also wanted and felt obligated to help the parents who seemed so upset and unhappy. When it was noted that she had a lot of feelings about all of this, tears came and she really showed her pain for the first time in the session. Until that point all feelings had been carefully tucked behind a sincere, vividly descriptive, but intellectual presentation. She tried quickly to regroup, laughingly noting that she is not depressed *all* 24 hours of the day—and besides, look at all she has learned: "I can now eat in a cafeteria with other people and I couldn't before." The hour ended with her agreeing that there were indeed things to sort out in her life, and it could be helpful to talk some more.

Sessions were planned for twice a week through the summer. The separation issues emerged dramatically in this first hour, cloaked only slightly by the presenting complaints of academic difficulties and social excesses. It was interesting that there was intellectual concern about these, but no discernible guilt. Jean could observe patterns well, although she as yet was unable to draw important connections. She was bright, verbal, and seemed curious. The therapist's goal for therapy was to prevent further regression and to help Jean with her goal of returning to school.

The next several visits centered around Jean's perceptions of her parents. Mother was described as warm, emotional, and dramatic, with advanced degrees in English and Theater Arts. She had recently studied accounting to please the father, a successful financier who also wanted Jean to go in this direction, even though her first love and apparent talent was in writing. Mother felt she had no place and no friends. Instead, she confided in Jean, seeking Jean's help in saving herself and her marriage. Sexual details and problems were openly revealed. In response to the comment that mother seemed to share quite a lot, the patient replied, "She's a peer, growing up with us. There are three girls and Daddy."

Father was Old World in style, with a boot-strap philosophy that ridiculed psychological, symbolic, and poetic ideas. He favored a tight value system governed by notions of discipline. He was unsympathetic to his wife's and daughter's therapies, and uncomfortable in his struggle with his three "nutty women," while his own male colleagues seemed to be comfortable in a chauvinistic lifestyle. He communicated with Jean only about his own sense of despair at his failure as a parent and as a husband. Jean felt she must listen, tacitly comfort, but never debate these matters with her father.

As the summer proceeded, the parents' relationship, never ideal, showed significant deterioration. There were the familiar lengthy family discussions. The scenes the patient described were numerous and increasingly upsetting. The patient felt loyally stuck in her role as rescuer to the mother and confidante to the father. There seemed, on the parents' part, no empathy for the daughter's conflict between her mother's world of ideas and her father's world of values and numbers.

Never was her own shaky college situation addressed nor her personal problems.

As Jean described the inflammatory situations at home, she seemed at first oblivious to their peculiar nature. The therapist listened, limiting comments to inquiries about how Jean herself felt, but showing honest reactions of surprise and dismay to the recitals of the erratic parental behavior. This may have helped Jean question her own passive acquiescence, and to view her parents in a new and different way.

Gradually, Jean was able to acknowledge her unrecognized anger at being caught in the middle and "used" by her parents. She recalled that friends had always said she never showed anger, and she figured she channeled it all against herself. It was agreed that therapy would concentrate on getting her back on track with her own life. She remembered that she had felt alone a lot growing up, but that father approved of her intellectual pursuits and mother delighted in her interest in writing—encouraging her to write the Definitive Play—and perhaps to have kids some day but to adopt them out and go on creating. She realized that her college boyfriend, a philosopher, "rambled" much like her mother and that this was what attracted her. He and philosophy became a replacement for the long discussions at home. She remembered a trip with mother at age eight when they went 200 miles out of the way while mother explained Lear—causes and effects—and she listened. "Most eight-year-olds would have been bored, and my sister couldn't sit through it, but I was fascinated, and mother was enchanted that she had captured my interest. I felt happy then, normal as long as I was at home. It was only outside the home I felt shy and different." The therapist commented how unusual her childhood must have been. Finally, Jean could experience some new and real anger at the unusual bonding with her mother. "I grew up on literary metaphors—I had no childhood."

While she remained somewhat more sympathetic to her father, she mobilized some resentment at his tendency to devalue the mother and all women, and saw her own "breaking loose" in college as a protest against his rigid and austere values as well as the more esoteric ones of her mother. The therapist continued to ask Jean about her own interests and continued to wonder how she might extricate herself in order to pursue them. Soon the patient reported being able to leave the worrisome and chaotic household she'd felt obliged to oversee to go occasionally to the library to work on her overdue papers. She began swimming regularly at a nearby pool, to get back into shape and to improve her body image, a move that was overdue.

While events at home still kept her distraught, and monopolized the therapy time, she was increasingly able to speak of her reactions and to express her feelings as to what was going on. With great effort, she was able to pull herself away from the intrigue at home and into an 18-year-old life. She called a friend, she went to a movie, she walked out on a particularly stormy parental scene, and she tried to study. Interestingly, her appearance began to change as she began to define her own boundaries. The wild hairdo and unkempt dress were modified—she actually looked more contained.

At the end of the first week in August, with three sessions remaining (during which the therapist had planned to deal with termination issues) Jean called to say she had been invited by a friend in Boston to come visit, and what should she do? She felt she needed to escape the increasing turmoil at home, but she feared losing her remaining therapy time and possibly risking the therapist's disapproval. This was reflected back to her and after some discussion and despite her mixed feelings, it was settled that she would go.

Jean was not seen again. The termination issues were not specifically talked about, but, in the phone transaction some things were in fact dealt with. Once again the need to be the good girl (good patient) loyally tied to the parent (therapist) surfaced. Although there was conflict, it seemed she felt encouraged to make her own choice, and given permission, as it were, to separate and go on.

A month later, Jean wrote the therapist that she had returned to school, felt better, and was studiously and defensively avoiding the pitfalls of the previous year until she felt better able to handle them. What she felt she had learned in therapy, essentially, was to be able to say no to unreasonable demands that threatened her own autonomy and individuality. She had even said no to her beloved sister's latest request to falsify a letter on her behalf, and had withstood her mother's desperate pleadings that she remain home. She experienced gratitude and was able to joke about her "genetic verbosity." Jean specifically said she needed no response to this letter and so it was left. Jean's treatment consisted of a total of 10 visits.

In a sense Jean demonstrates a rather difficult problem of separation, complicated by the parents' marital difficulties and the behavior of Jean's sister. It was of sufficient seriousness that open-ended psychotherapy was undertaken.

In the first session with Jean, several things were noted that would bear upon the therapy. Foremost was that she presented, as many college students do, as bright, verbal, and observing, but fairly oblivious to the idea that her behavior might have meaning and that meaning could be understood. The therapist's immediate posture of wondering why she thought certain things had happened invited the student to join in the inquiry and to scrutinize herself (and in this case, her family as well) in some fresh ways.

It was also clear that much of her affect was hidden even to herself. The therapist asked specifically and repeatedly about feelings, thereby encouraging the student to experience and discuss them, rather than putting so much into actions, which were less accessible to understanding.

While the student acknowledged readily her deep wishes to please her parents, she was largely unaware that the need to please also represented an attachment and dependency that was difficult to give up. She was also unaware of the competition and the identification with her sister, and the vicarious pleasure and imagined freedoms she gained through the sister rather than herself. These dynamics needed only occasionally to be interpreted in so many words to Jean. Rather, the therapist chose to encourage and assist the development of the student's own insights, offering appropriate agreement or support as her understanding widened.

The therapist actively encouraged independence, particularly in self, peer, and education directed activities.

As the description flowed regarding the parents' sometimes

chaotic behavior, the therapist's largely affectual communication (a "Really!", a gasp, a raised eyebrow) permitted the patient to begin viewing the parental behavior with her own more adult rational instruments rather than through the tinted glasses of the devoted child who denied anything could be amiss with the needed parental figures. This conflict was interpreted and was also relived in the transference experience.

The therapist was alert to the impulse to want to rescue the student in response to the clear, but nonverbal, transference wish of the student to find a parent in the therapist. This nonverbal interaction was not directly interpreted but was reflected in the student's tendency to want to be a "good" patient, and obliquely addressed in the phone call that encouraged her toward resolution and growth. Furthermore, the therapist subtly encouraged Jean to establish peer relationships to replace the original family. The therapist supported progressive developmental movement by concentrating therapeutic interventions away from the family and toward resolving anxieties that could interfere with the development of new peer relationships even at the cost of stopping therapy earlier than the agreed-upon date.

Grace was a 21-year-old college senior. Both her parents were professionals in another city. She was a capable student at a major university, heading for a career. She was referred for therapy because she had become depressed following an acute family crisis over the summer. In the past, she had had several periods of treatment with a therapist whom she called by her first name and who lived in a neighboring town.

Grace's father was a successful businessman, very involved with his public image. There had been considerable ongoing marital tension between the parents. The father was narcissistic, highly invested in his own work, and critical of the mother and her professional activities. Mother, on the other hand, paid little explicit attention to his achievements and recognition, feeling that these were escapes from contact with people and from the family.

The incident that precipitated the daughter's depression was the announcement by her one-year-older brother that he intended to get married. The brother had been a close confidante. Although now attending another university, he had taken a year off from college so brother and sister were graduating at the same time. It was clear that in many ways he had replaced her rather unavailable and remote father and that when he announced his engagement, she felt that she had lost him to another woman. She was managing these angry feelings and sense of loss by alternately seeking contact with him and repulsing any attempt he made to call her or speak to her, leaving him alienated and confused.

She felt extremely angry, tearful, unable to work or to continue her involvement with her roommates with whom she had very long-standing, close, and good friendships. She also regretted that because of her depression, she was not able to make full use of the opportunities her senior year offered for friendships and for serious work on a thesis that she had planned to enjoy. She had a boyfriend whom she had known for about a year, with whom things were up and down. Both the boyfriend and her brother were applying to competitive graduate schools. They were both high achievers, similar to her father, and in some ways, quite competitive. She herself recognized that she disliked the pattern, but was drawn to people who were similar to her father.

The first phase of treatment consisted of addressing her immediate depression and inability to work. The therapist was very active. The history made it clear that her relationship with her brother was also a substitute for an unfulfilled longing for closeness with her father. The therapist then discussed Grace's relationship with her father. Grace was perceptive, and in her family there was considerable discussion of personal interactions and feelings, even though the father seemed remarkably insensitive to the real effects of his behavior on his children. While crying, the patient related that he rarely called her. When she called the family, which she usually did right after 11:00 because the rates were cheaper, he would say "hello" perfunctorily, and then say he wanted to watch his favorite television program. Although angry with him, she clearly wanted to please him. At other times they would talk freely about a number of issues. He would ask about her academic achievements and her personal life, including sex and her relationship with her boyfriend, but his self-involvement and difficulty in being empathic with her were clear. She wanted to feel that she had something that she could teach him or offer him. He had turned to her brother various times because the brother had some specific mathematical and computer skills, which the father valued, and she had felt devalued by this preference.

Academic achievement was extremely important in this family, as was a kind of exaggerated emotional interchange, which had all the earmarks of communication, but Grace at least felt that she wasn't really listened to by her father. The therapist worked actively on Grace's feelings of anger, abandonment, longing, resentment of her brother, and the relationship of these feelings to her feelings about her father. Her brother's fiancee seemed "ordinary" to Grace, and although she recognized that this woman was appropriate for her brother, she also felt displaced and devalued by his choice.

This first phase of treatment lasted a month, and also involved arrangements about the Thanksgiving vacation. She was hesitant to join the family during a planned trip. She described the events of the summer in which she had gone away with her family, had found she could not tolerate it, and had left after a day. This whole fashion of behaving was very unlike her usual self. She generally presented a cheerful self to the world, while at the same time she resented that she was always expected to be cheerful.

The therapist suggested that Grace try to communicate to her brother her feelings of anger and sadness at the change in their relationship. She decided to write him a long letter. After she wrote and mailed it, he called her, and after the phone conversation, there was a marked change in her mood. She felt immensely relieved, able to communicate with him and to explain some of the puzzling resentments and rejections, which he had really not understood.

Things seemed to be settling down. She applied to graduate school, began her senior thesis, and applied for a prestigious scholarship. She was angry that her father seemed more interested in the scholarship than anything else, but nevertheless she seemed to feel better, and for a while considered terminating treatment. She skipped a therapy session; but when her boyfriend responded to her ambivalence and put some pressure on her, she again became depressed and therapy resumed.

The next phase involved working through some of her feelings about her boyfriend. She recognized that she would probably not stay with him after they entered graduate school. The anxiety of the application process for them both and the subsequent waiting period dominated this phase. The therapist was supportive and also encouraged examining some of the specific aspects of her relationship with her boyfriend. One of their major difficulties was his sexism, which she resented. There were also problems in their sexual relationship; it seemed as if his self-esteem was dependent on her sexual interest in him, which was frequently low. She was puzzled by this and recognized that it seemed to her at times that she was "being used" to provide an orgasm for him. There were times when she didn't feel like having sex. Nevertheless, she didn't really want to lose him so they patched things up. She resumed her relationships with her roommates, whom she really seemed to care for a great deal. Two of them were also applying to graduate schools, and they were clearly a very able group.

The next phase of treatment was precipitated by Grace's parents' unexpected announcement shortly after Christmas vacation that they were going to separate. She was in tears about this, and the therapist again worked actively to explore her feelings about the break-up of her family at a time that she was entering a new phase of her own life. In addition to the fact of their separation, she resented the way that they were going about it. She thought their proposed arrangements were bizarre, but could neither clarify for herself her father's childish behavior, nor her mother's masochism in putting up with it. She was angry with them, found it difficult to communicate with them, and responded to them as she had to her brother. She had conscious feelings of longing for a kind of ordinary intimate relationship with them, especially with her mother, but also wished to avoid hearing discussions of the fluctuations in their feelings. Gradually this phase was resolved as her parents' relationship settled down somewhat. She was angry with her mother for putting up with her father's criticisms and putdowns for so many years. She was also critical of her mother for wanting a reconciliation after an initial phase of relief stemming from the fact that the father's constant criticism was absent. Grace felt her mother demeaned herself by such a change of heart.

In the meantime, Grace was accepted to several graduate schools, made a visit to at least two of them, and found one that she liked. She was waiting to hear from one other, but she had a good choice. Both her brother and her boyfriend also had some prestigious acceptances, as did her girlfriends. She, her brother, and boyfriend were all considering alternatives.

Treatment ended with her graduation, although many unresolved issues remained regarding her relationships both with her parents and with men.

She was able to define major residual therapeutic issues. She recognized that she was attracted to men who had the same characterological style and problems as her father. Although they might provide a way to gain closeness to her father, she would probably reexperience the frustrations that she had felt with him. Her actual relationship with her father improved, but its stability is difficult to predict until her parents reach a stable marital arrangement. She was also aware of unresolved issues and contradictions in her sexual feelings, which would require further exploration.

The therapist's willingness to be active and interpretive, as well as to be supportive, in the initial phase was an important aspect of the treatment. The therapist made considerable efforts to point out that Grace's reaction to her brother's engagement was a displacement of the reaction to her father, as well as constituting a loss in its own right. The therapist also emphasized the developmental and maturational potential of this event, although the resulting gain was achieved at considerable cost and suffering. The therapist made the active suggestion that Grace try to establish communication with her brother. Important in her feeling of being helped was the therapist's acknowledgment that Grace had both the "right to feel bad and that this was a time of particular difficulty for many young people." Grace had been having trouble with the fact that no one in her family really saw this as a time of particular stress for her and consequently couldn't understand her reactions. Her brother seemed to be weathering it with more calm and isolation, although he too seemed somewhat troubled, initially.

This case illustrates the constraints of time, the impact of semester breaks, and the prominence of school issues. It also illustrates how a therapist can take an active stance because of the immediate requirements of the situation and can then step back into a more exploratory and analytic mode when the crisis is over. There is no question that further therapeutic work would be helpful to this student. In this context, the underlying issue of her relationship with her father and brother was only touched on, and almost no work was done on the expression of her sexual feelings. However, further exploration was not urgent at the time she sought therapy and the major goal of helping her reestablish her ability to function was accomplished. Her presenting symptoms were resolved and she completed her academic requirements within the necessary time frame. The realities of the school schedule and imminent graduation made further exploration impossible and not really appropriate. It was suggested as a possibility for the future.

SUMMARY

To conduct effective psychotherapy with college students is basically to conduct good psychotherapy. However, when working with college students, there are certain unique characteristics that must be kept in mind.

First, most college students are in the last phase of adolescent development; and while it is appropriate to respond to them as young adults, one must not overlook the fact that they are still in the process of emotional and psychological change. Because of this, therapeutic interventions can frequently be brief or discontinuous. In fact, longer term therapy may actually be contraindicated, although the therapist needs to maintain a degree of openmindedness about the matter.

Second, the college calendar and environment impose certain constraints on the student's life. It is important for the therapist to be aware of these, because they may have a significant influence on the student's current experience and the type of emotional problems that may bring a student to therapy. An understanding of the progression through college may be extremely useful in providing the student with the most rapid and effective kind of help.

Third, the college student, intelligent, eager to explore, and verbal, can be a stimulating patient to treat in psychotherapy; furthermore, the student is often describing experience evocative of the therapist's own. For both these reasons there may be complex countertransference issues. The therapist must be alert to these, or the therapy may bog down. On the other hand, the therapist may be able to use countertransference feelings creatively.

Fourth, while psychotherapy with college students follows basic therapeutic principles, there are additional unique aspects. For example, a more interactive mode is required, with emphasis on current conflicts as they relate to developmental tasks, and early termination may be more reflective of burgeoning autonomy than mere resistance to therapy. Recognition of these unique aspects may contribute much to successful therapy with college students.

When the above considerations are properly attended to, therapy can be immensely helpful for the student.

7

SOME SPECIAL STUDENT POPULATIONS

In Chapter 5 we described the issues that must be considered in the psychological assessment of a college student. These include the thoughtful overall psychiatric evaluation required for any person in distress and, in addition, a heightened awareness of the developmental stage of late adolescence with its varied and complex manifestations of conflict. Such assessment must also address the setting in which students are living while grappling with the tasks of growing up and attempting to consolidate their identity. In this chapter we will discuss some special considerations that may play a part in the maturational process.

First, we will consider some of the unique features and needs of a few specific populations in the college community. It would be impossible to deal comprehensively with all groups, but perhaps citing some examples will serve to emphasize the importance of being attentive to small and large historical clues, as students seek help with their current conscious concerns.

The therapist will derive these "clues" from many different sources. In the following material we address those clues that may accrue from the student's particular background. While we are categorizing "background" in subgroups in order to emphasize special aspects to be noted and respected, the central issue is individuality. Each student presents with a unique conglomerate of assets and vulnerabilities which are multi-determined. Each student deserves the fullest appreciation of self and a fair evaluation of the many determinants that have played a part in that individual's development to date. The following discussions, then, emphasize some factors that should be understood by a therapist as possible important contributing elements, but that in no way define any single individual.

Differences of age, class, race, and ethnic background may evoke unique problems and become issues in a student's view of self and others in the college setting. In the adolescent years, the struggle to accept oneself, to achieve independence, and at the same time to find acceptance in a group to which one wishes to belong are critical. Thus, the student's sociocultural background will affect the experience and resolution of the dominant conflicts of this period. These strivings may be more poignant and often more difficult for students with special backgrounds.

Earlier life experiences contribute to a variety of assumptions and expectations which students bring to the college environment. These assumptions, in turn, may generate attitudes and behaviors that may or may not be correctly understood by student peers or by the important adults whom students will encounter. Most people tend to adhere tenaciously to the belief system held by the group with which they identify; as a result, misunderstanding between members of differing groups is fairly universal.

FIRST PERSON IN A FAMILY TO ATTEND COLLEGE

Students from working class backgrounds who are the first in their families to attend college usually come with the task of needing to succeed, not only for themselves but for their family, and sometimes for a whole community. That in itself can be a huge burden, leaving little or no room for the student's own interests, timetable, or needs. Such students may feel constrained to waste no time in completing their degree. In addition to carrying a full academic load, they often have to work during the semester in order to make ends meet; and summers may be spent with unsatisfying jobs that are necessary to help pay for the tuition or living expenses of the subsequent semester. It is not unusual for these students to feel "burned out" by junior or senior year.

Furthermore, such students do not have the almost automatic backing and understanding found in families whose members have been to college and know about the experience. It is ironic to see someone who is sent to "succeed," who then becomes interested in an "esoteric" subject such as ancient art history, and who is consequently misunderstood or criticized by parents who urge a more "practical" course of study, such as engineering or business. Such students, whose families do not value abstract thinking, reading, or intellectual endeavor, are caught in a predicament. They confront not only the challenges of a new environment and academic requirements, but also the realization that the further they advance, the more successful in their academic work and the greater their intellectual growth, the more alienated they become from their families. The result is a painful conflict which complicates normal individuation.

Alex, a junior, sought treatment for a moderately severe depression. He gave a history that included some phobic symptoms in his past two years of college. His fears had gradually subsided, but seemed to have been replaced by the depression that brought him to the student health center. As he talked, it became fairly clear that both sets of symptoms involved his relationship with his family.

He came from a small Midwestern town that was dominated by a large industrial plant where his father worked as a foreman. His mother occasionally worked as a clerk, although most of her time was spent as a homemaker. No one in the family had ever been to college. In high school, Alex was an outstanding athlete and a good student. He had hoped to attend a service academy, but his chances were defeated by a labile blood pressure condition. Because of his athletic achievements, he came to the attention of one of the plant executives, who urged him to apply to the executive's alma mater. He did so and was accepted.

Although he was pleased at the prospect of attending the

college, it was some distance from home, and he had considerable difficulty with separation from his family. As he became more comfortable at college, however, he found himself drifting further from his family. A crisis occurred when he chose to major in history. He remarked that to his family, history was the equivalent of majoring in mythology, and they could neither understand nor approve his choice. Although he was happy with his major, he found himself inexplicably becoming depressed.

He was aware that, unlike his athletic achievements, he could not share his new interests or his new way of looking at current events with his family. He was drifting away from them in a way he feared would become unbridgeable. He understood his dilemma, but could see no way out of it. Speaking to a therapist who understood and discussed this dilemma with him helped the depression—though of course he was left to deal with the widening gulf between his family and the person he was becoming.

AFRICAN-AMERICAN STUDENTS

African-American students often carry the conscious or unconscious burden of the history of enslavement and segregation. As members of a separate group, previously excluded from public social interaction, they are often still perceived by the white population as different, inferior, and socially unacceptable. Consequently, young Blacks may come to see themselves in the same way, may develop a negative self-image, and may maintain an expectation of certain disapproval or defeat. Some, however, may defensively adopt arrogant postures, protesting anticipated inequities and proclaiming an aggressive superiority. As more African-American students from integrated neighborhoods or schools arrive at college, many will be increasingly comfortable in a racially mixed environment. Others will still suffer inwardly and continue to harbor doubts about themselves and fears of nonacceptance.

All students need friends and wish to avoid isolation. For some Blacks, there is a tendency to group together with other

Blacks. This may provide a sense of belonging and an umbrella of safety from expected hurt, but it may also limit the student's ability to feel identified with the student body at large and to become involved in college life. Furthermore, the presence of all-Black groups may be misconstrued by other students as hostility or indifference. The larger student body may then turn away, tending to confirm the minority student's expectation of rejection.

Some African-American students essentially deny differences and attempt to assimilate within the larger group. This is often accepted and successful. However, in some situations, the student is then viewed suspiciously by both groups—as a traitor by the one, as an impostor by the other. Such an individual feels accepted by neither, and must combat internal loneliness and despair.

African-American students may also face the bewildering loss of individuality that results when, as individuals coming from disparate social class backgrounds and having in common only their race, they are somehow perceived as indistinguishable. Thus, the urban affluent preparatory school offspring of Black professional parents may be viewed as similar to the economically and culturally deprived son or daughter of an impoverished farmer whose life experiences have never gone beyond a tiny rural ghetto. While such young people may indeed feel a certain "brotherhood" born of race and minority status, they are often totally different in personality, experience, and academic and social preparedness. If others ignore such legitimate differences, confusion, distress, and a diminished sense of self may result for both students.

The African-American student is often susceptible to certain additional emotional injuries that other students are less likely to incur.

Patricia and Marie met as freshmen in the same dorm. Both were from New York, daughters of caring, well-educated, ambitious parents. Both were attractive, bright, and sports minded. In background, interest, and style they shared much in common. Pat was a tall blonde of English descent; Marie was a willowy Black of mixed heritage. They became friends, dormmates sophomore year, and suitemates again in their junior year, when they moved together with six other close friends to a freshman dorm where the eight women would serve as junior advisers. The two best friends happily arranged their rooms with one as a sitting room and one for sleeping. This arrangement continued until spring, when Marie returned late one day from the lab to find the suite rearranged into separate bedrooms. Shocked and hurt, she looked around for Pat or some explanation, and found a letter lying open and obvious on Pat's desk. It was a sincerely worded, worried letter from Pat's parents urging her to re-evaluate her intense friendship, to think cautiously about her future in her own world. They suggested firmly that the close friendship with a "colored" person might not be in her best social interests. The two young women were never able to confront openly what had happened; they remained friends, but the painful secret between them inevitably altered their friendship in a permanent way.

African-American students, already sensitive to prejudices, are often vulnerable to slights, small or large, real or imagined, which may add to their mistrust of others or may damage their self-esteem. Clearly, this state of mind can affect their willingness to experiment with new behaviors and ideas and can influence how they proceed with the psychological developmental tasks of separation and individuation.

Finally, the African-American student may have special difficulties when seeking help at the health service. This is particularly likely if there are no Black therapists on the staff, or if the White therapists are either intimidated by, or ignorant of, some of the student's special concerns. The Black student is in the midst of the same developmental struggles as other students and will probably respond with least suspicion if race is neither ignored nor overemphasized. Directness, activity, and candor on the part of the therapist will facilitate the development of trust. Some feel that a non-White therapist is essential for work with a Black student to maximize the student's hope to be understood, and to serve as role model; most believe that well-trained, aware, and respectful White therapists, who have come to terms with their own racial attitudes, can usually establish an atmosphere of friendly, neutral inquiry and concern. A White therapist may even provide the Black student with an important experience in acceptance and connection.

NATIVE AMERICAN STUDENTS

Native American students are a varied group. As Marsh (1989) states, there are differences from one nation to another nation, differences between students who live in urban and rural areas, and between those who live on reservations and in nonreservation communities. For students who attend a college in a state where their tribe has large land holdings, it is easier to maintain cultural identity and retain a sense that "I can go back," for political, tribal and family events. This is different for Native Americans coming from small reservations, or from parts of the country where Native Americans are more deeply acculturated into the Anglo society. For example, urban (nonreservation) students often act and think in Anglo ways: They have learned to be assertive, to maintain eye contact, to ask many questions, to search out solutions for their needs. For students coming from a reservation, using such "coping skills" would be labeled "rude behavior." The more traditional Native American, on the other hand, may face the difficult task of learning how to acquire such "coping skills" for use in the university or the Anglo society at large, and yet be able to put aside such characteristics and return to traditional values when with other Native American friends or when back on the reservation. There are also difficulties for some in trying to acquire assertiveness skills at age 18, as opposed to having been implicitly taught such skills from early life.

Getting a good education may not be emphasized as directly as it sometimes is in Anglo society. Encouragement for education may be more indirect—education is good, but tribal/ personal values are primary. There may be pressure to attend college and get an education, counterposed against pressure to not graduate. This ambivalence stems from recognition by

Native Americans that becoming educated is the way to get ahead, countervailed by the fear that once someone has graduated he or she will leave the reservation for good.

A Native American who has attended reservation schools, or Bureau of Indian Affairs schools, is less likely to have been exposed to a college preparatory curriculum than students from public schools. Transition to college by way of junior college may then be important for students gradually to move into the more demanding university or college environment, an environment which assumes a certain mastery of various study skills. Even then, keeping up academically may be a struggle.

For many Native Americans, whatever difficulty their minority status entails is compounded by the fact that they are likely to be the first in their families to leave home and attend college.

Important reasons for Native Americans dropping out of school include social adjustment, academics, and difficulty in telling anyone, in particular mental health specialists, that they are having a problem. In addition to the cultural differences, our country's historical treatment of Native Americans adds to the wary avoidance of Anglo professional services.

Acculturated Native American students who have been more successful in temporarily adopting the Anglo coping skills are more likely to seek help. More traditional students return home for a ceremony or consultation with a native healer when they are experiencing what others would call a mental health problem.

ASIAN-AMERICAN STUDENTS

Asian-American students are designated as having minority status although many Asian-American individuals do not so regard themselves. Thus, the fact that an institution treats them as a minority can be confusing. The term "Asian-American" includes individuals who can be first or second generation and who stem from a variety of distinct cultural backgrounds. Nonetheless, on campus, members of this diverse population tend to be classified as a single group, which undoubtedly creates confusion. Asian-Americans come from many disparate cultures, often with strong nationalistic feelings, and each with its own customs, mores, and beliefs. An incomplete list, for example, would include mainland Chinese, Taiwanese, Japanese, Thai, Korean, Vietnamese, Laotians, Cambodians, and Filipinos. Some have been assimilated as Americans, some may be recent immigrants who still have difficulty speaking and understanding the language. As a result, identity conflicts frequently contribute to anxiety and emotional tension.

As with all groups, any generalizations are questionable, and frequently negated by exceptions. Collectively, however, on the campus, Asian-Americans have been regarded as ambitious, highly motivated, excellent students. Accordingly, many of the special programs that have been established in the belief that "minority students" have suffered past academic deprivation are not appropriate for this group. Family values emphasize academic performance, and any failure to live up to expectations may lead to depression; this is often denied but may become manifest in the form of physical symptoms. As a corollary, the time and effort that Asian-American students have expended on their studies may cause them to be less experienced socially, and in the freer college atmosphere, they may feel lonely or inadequate. Cultural values they bring with them may minimize the importance of feelings and tend to characterize any emotional difficulty as "weakness" rather than as illness (Martinez et al., 1989). These attitudes often result in a reluctance to obtain professional help.

> James was an Asian-American freshman from Southern California who matriculated at a selective college on the Eastern seaboard. Referral to the mental health service was suggested in November by a nurse after he had presented with stomach pains that seemed without organic basis. He agreed reluctantly. When seen by a psychiatrist, he stated that he had been "feeling low" ever since arriving on campus. Seeing the psychiatrist was not easy for him, however, because he wondered what people would think about him if they knew he was "weak enough" to need psychiatric help. He spoke of feeling

lonely and of missing his friends, and especially his girlfriend at home. Although he was not failing his courses, he was not getting A's, and he found this very frustrating.

Since coming to college he was increasingly concerned about his ethnicity. Where he grew up he never thought about being a minority individual, but at college he felt that he had experienced both overt and covert prejudice. He had not been asked to join a fraternity, and he noted that there were only one or two Asian-Americans in the fraternities. Most of his friendships were with other Asian-American students, and he felt alienated from the non-Asian students. Specifically, he felt that his roommate, who was from a wealthy Northeastern suburb, was uncomfortable with him.

James did exceedingly well in high school and was a merit scholar. He was attracted to his chosen college by its traditions. Once on campus, however, he felt that the traditions failed to include minority students. He was also concerned about the expense to his family. He stated that his family was close, and he missed them greatly. He was concerned about disappointing them academically, although they denied that they expected high performance from him.

Psychotherapy was recommended because the therapist felt that it might be helpful for him to explore identity issues. However, James was concerned about confidentiality, and was worried that being in therapy might affect his career. He was given some direct reassurance and asked to call back if his symptoms persisted, but the therapist felt that he probably would not accept the recommendation for further help.

This student could have benefited from psychotherapy, but the therapist was not able to overcome the student's reluctance, which was in part culturally derived.

HISPANIC-AMERICAN STUDENTS

Like Asian-Americans, the Hispanic minority consists of students from different cultural backgrounds, and, as such, should not be considered as a homogeneous group. The largest subgroups are mainland Puerto Ricans and Mexican-

Americans (Chicanos), followed by island Puerto Ricans and Cubans. As with African-Americans and Asian-Americans, however, within these subgroups there are wide variations in socioeconomic status so that pre-college experience may differ greatly. All may have had some exposure to bilingualism, but, again, the impact this has had on the individual student will vary.

Furthermore, inasmuch as some Hispanic-American subgroups tend to be concentrated in specific geographical areas, such as Mexican-Americans in the Southwest and Cubans in Florida, depending on the choice of college, the student may be close to home with nearby family who can provide support, or at some distance and isolated.

Whether there is a discernible "Latin temperament" that influences the reactions and interactions of Hispanic students is questionable, but the following case vignette describes a student who saw herself in that light.

Maria, a sophomore of Hispanic descent, was initially seen because of depression, which, in addition to being distressing, interfered with her ability to complete her academic work. She went to the medical clinic thinking that there might be some physical ailment. She was referred to the mental health service for evaluation and treatment of her depression. When seen in initial evaluation, she stated that for the past two weeks she had been under stress, was losing interest in her schoolwork, and had missed several classes. As a minority student on a work study program, she felt considerable pressure to achieve, and often took on more work than she could handle.

She began psychotherapy, and it soon became apparent that she had deeper problems, which would not be resolved by short-term work. Many of these involved past conflicts with her family and, in particular, a difficult relationship with her father. The therapy was unquestionably influenced by her frequent outbursts of intense effect, which she ascribed to her Hispanic background and to her "Latino temperament." However, her presentation went beyond cultural appro-

priateness and was felt to represent borderline symptomatology. With the help of several successive therapists who provided support during her upper class years, she eventually
managed to finish her degree and graduate.

In addition to providing medication and general support,
the therapy was helpful in allowing her to discuss her conflicts
about her minority status. She expressed difficulty in dealing
with two different cultures as she moved from home to college
and back. In all probability, however, the therapy did not
succeed in resolving her underlying disorder.

YOUNGER STUDENTS

Although most special programs encouraging early matriculation at college have been ended, there are still a certain number
of students who enter college at an age significantly younger
than the usual range. Characteristically, these are students who
are extremely capable intellectually, but who are emotionally
less ready to deal with college life. Many are able to make the
adjustment to college and confront the developmental tasks at
an earlier age. For others, two possible consequences ensue: If
they are at a residential college, they may find themselves
excluded from social activities and/or picked on and teased,
leading to considerable unhappiness, isolation, and loneliness.
Or, if they look physically the age of other students, they may
find themselves involved in situations they cannot handle emotionally and may become anxious or depressed, or even, in
reaction to these feeling states, overactive in social activities and
inappropriate in their behaviors.

Seth came to the college of his choice at the age of 16. He had
been a star student in the sciences at a suburban high school
with a good academic record, and he saw no reason to postpone college as was suggested by the high school college
advisor. When he reached college, he found himself behind
in his social experience, and in an attempt to buttress his
somewhat deflated sense of self-esteem, he began to fantasize

experiences with women, which he reported to roommates as fact. Gradually, the dividing line between fact and fantasy became less clear, and he began to develop stories about illnesses occurring among his relatives in an effort to elicit sympathy as a "tragic figure." This information began to worry his roommates, and they discussed their concerns with their residence hall advisor. This senior student met with Seth several times. As it became clearer that Seth's distress was a result of low self-esteem and anxiety, the residence hall advisor was able to be supportive, to question sensitively the apparent lying behavior, and then to facilitate a referral to the mental health service for evaluation.

Although initially embarrassed and taken aback by being "found out," Seth did follow through with his appointments. He used the supportive relationship with his therapist to better understand his current dilemma. He considered withdrawing from school. He was surprised but pleased that his parents understood what he was going through and expressed support for any decision he would make regarding school and also for his continuing in therapy. After several weeks, Seth commented that he had made the right decision about coming to college. He was feeling much better about himself and his relationships. There was now a group of male friends with whom he shared common interests, and several women he liked whom he had met at the Student Union film committee meetings. He said that he had "decided to go with the flow" and did not feel under pressure to be in an intense sexual relationship to prove something. He and his therapist made the decision to continue regular meetings, as his focus broadened to include concerns about family issues and some distress about procrastination and perfectionism.

This student's academic strength was not sufficient to sustain his self-confidence when he began to feel inadequate socially. He reacted to the latter feeling by reporting imaginary experience as real. Although inflating sexual exploits is a very common practice among adolescent males, Seth's fantasies multiplied and the line between reality and fantasy became blurred.

A more mature student would probably have been able to find better ways of combatting a feeling of inadequacy.

OLDER STUDENTS

Older students usually come to college after having had experiences that involve responsibility, such as holding a job, or being a housewife and mother. They are accustomed to some independence and have had experience in the ways of the world. They may be more tolerant of ambiguity and may have the support of a spouse. These advantages, however, may create problems for the older student; the transition may involve giving up an important and respected position and trading some power and autonomy for the more ambiguous and, at times, subservient position of student (Johnson & Schwartz, 1989).

Such older students may feel denigrated by professors who assume they have limited worldly experience and know as little as the remainder of the class. Being out of phase with peers, perhaps even having children the same age as their classmates, may cause unresolved adolescent problems to resurface. This can be unnerving and can bring an older student to treatment.

> Charlotte was approaching 50 when she decided she needed to do more with her life. She was the wife of a businessman, mother of three adult children who were married, thriving in their careers, and living at some distance from their parents. She herself had been active in school and community affairs for many years and had been a working president of an important Board of Directors. Except for that executive role, her efforts at home and outside had been largely of a caretaking nature, which she enjoyed and which reflected her upbringing as the daughter of a small-town minister. She was well-read and enjoyed writing poetry and prose. She therefore determined to pursue courses in English in order to complete her degree. This had been interrupted after her sophomore year because at the time she felt she had no real direction.

Her first encounter with anxiety centered around the writing of a personal essay for the college application. It was inexplicable to her that tracing her own history should cause such tension. Some months later, accepted by the local college and preparing her first composition assignment, she again experienced intense and debilitating anxiety, severe enough to imperil her academic status, even before it had fully begun. It was at that point that she sought help. It soon emerged in therapy that, in reviewing her adolescence for the essay, she recalled profound suppressed conflicts around sexuality, and abuse by an older brother when she was very young. These issues led to a longer, more intense psychotherapy than most older students require when the anxiety does not connect to such extremely traumatic earlier events.

There may be significant conflicts because of responsibilities, which inevitably interfere with studying. The older student will probably need more money for living expenses and may need to have outside jobs. Opportunity to participate in college activities will be limited. The older student may feel further distanced on a residential campus where so much of the living and learning experience and sense of community involves extracurricular activities for which these students may have neither interest nor time. If the older student is a woman who has lost a marital partner, she may feel it necessary to learn more in order to earn more. While highly motivated, these women are often still suffering a sense of loss, loneliness, and dislocation in their lives.

Nancy eloped when she was very young, just months after her twin sister married. Her husband's career gradually prospered, and she was able to raise their two children in a lifestyle far more luxurious than she had known in her own childhood. She directed the entertainment and vacations and mastered the sports of riding, skiing, and golf. While she felt herself fortunate in her choice of mate, she believed her own contribution to their success had been substantial. She was devastated, therefore, to learn her husband was leaving her for a younger woman. There was a period of compulsive and histrionic protest, which later she felt embarrassed about, but as it became clear that her life was no longer merged with her partner's, she became worried about her future.

Her sister, mother, and college-aged daughter urged her to obtain more education, as there was the real possibility that her ex-husband would not entirely support her. Angry, jealous, and desperate, she enrolled in college. Her first disappointment was the alienation she felt from the jeans-clad young students in her classes. She learned to leave her designer wardrobe and fashionable car behind. Even more sobering was the disparity she felt between herself and the other students in language and general knowledge. When her attempts to mother, befriend, or bribe classmates failed, she felt herself a total failure and sought help because of serious feelings of depression.

It was soon clear that this woman might some day benefit from long-term therapy. Before she became a satellite to her husband, she had been a satellite to her more dominant twin. The more immediate task in treatment, however, was to help her reestablish sufficient self-esteem to enable her to experience some pleasure and confidence in making choices for herself. Within three sessions, the patient realized how even the decision to enter college, while a reasonable one in some ways, was made in response to the ideas of others. She felt that she really was not immediately interested in academics, but rather wanted to put her life together in some other way. Having recognized this, she quit college, took a 12-week course in travel advising, and got a job in a travel agency. Some months later she wrote her therapist from Florida to say she was doing well and had begun psychotherapy.

This brief therapy allowed the student-patient to realize that college is not the answer to every situation and that the decision to enroll was not the correct one for her.

MARRIED STUDENTS

With the increase in older individuals attending college and the not infrequent postponement of an individual's matriculation because of career uncertainty or the need to earn some money, married undergraduates, while still a minority on campus, exist and often are involved in conflict that brings them to therapy either individually or as a couple. Sometimes the difficulty involves resentment by the nonstudent, who may be working to support the couple, while the spouse "is sitting around doing nothing." If the nonstudent is the wife, this resentment may be increased by the fact that she is typically expected to do the housework as well as hold a full-time, paid job. In other circumstances, the couple's relationship may be negatively affected by changes in their individual developments that presumably could occur even if one member of the couple were not in college as the following vignette illustrates.

Beth and Lance, both 25, sought couples therapy. They had been married for two years, but had been going steady since they were 16. They had initially attended the same high school and fallen in love when they were both juniors. Although they had intended to marry from early in their relationship, Lance was uncertain about his career direction, and he elected to take a job as a construction worker for two years prior to matriculating at college. Beth, meanwhile, had gone on to college so that she completed her B.A. as Lance was finishing his sophomore year. She then took a job in an insurance agency, which she saw as a way of marking time until Lance completed college. They had postponed making firm decisions about their future careers, but she did hope to go on to graduate school.

Tensions began to increase at the end of Lance's junior year, and became more intense at the beginning of his senior year, with frequent explosive arguments or periods of silence and avoiding interaction. Beth brought up the possibility of a trial separation, and some resolution seemed essential. Beth described the problem as a lack of communication and an unwillingness on Lance's part to discuss what she saw as "important decisions," while Lance felt that "matters would eventually solve themselves" and indicated that "he did not like confrontation." Their differences extended to their sexual relationship, which at one time had been active and satisfying, but had gradually become rather desultory and, according to Beth, lacking in emotion.

This vignette illustrates a relationship that began when both individuals were quite young, and probably still somewhat unformed, so the initial basis for attraction to each other changed as each matured. Although the college experience itself may have had little impact on the maturing process, and similar difficulties might have arisen if neither had entered college, the decisions that generally must be considered in the process of progress through college unquestionably intensified the underlying conflicts.

SINGLE-PARENT STUDENTS

It is not unusual for older divorced women to return to college to complete a degree. In addition to all the adjustments this choice will entail as an older student, having to care for dependent children at home obviously adds significant additional responsibilities and burdens. A younger student may face similar experiences. Because women students who become pregnant, whether or not married, often decide to interrupt their education in order to care for the baby initially on a full-time basis, it is not unusual for them to attempt to return to college when the baby is a toddler or slightly older. If the father is not in the picture, the mother as a single parent (or for that matter the father, although men less often have custody when the child is young) must cope with problems of child care, as well as provision of financial support, and the pressure of academic work. Although many of the resulting difficulties are practical ones, the mixture of responsibilities can have an emotional impact as well.

Naomi had become pregnant during sophomore year after an intense whirlwind romance lasting a month, which began to cool about the time that she missed her period. When the pregnancy was confirmed, her boyfriend showed no interest in marriage and urged her to obtain an abortion. Although she considered the idea, it was against her religious beliefs, and she decided to carry to term and to raise the child herself, as some of her older cousins, not college students, had done. She managed to finish her sophomore year, but decided that she wanted to devote her time exclusively to the baby, so she took a leave of absence from college.

After a year of motherhood, she felt that she was ready to return to college. She was fortunate in being able to arrange for good day care, but her return to college was accompanied by feelings that she had not anticipated. She found herself quite envious of the freedom her classmates had—a freedom that she had taken for granted before. And, although she enjoyed being with her child, she found the problem of managing her time more difficult than she had anticipated. At a point when she began to feel some resentment toward her child, she became frightened and discussed her situation with her pediatrician who referred her for evaluation and possible therapy.

This vignette simply illustrates that it is sometimes more difficult to combine parental and academic responsibilities than one anticipates. Furthermore, the wish for some kind of adult romantic relationship can act as an additional pressure or source of depression and can cause the student to contrast her current state with her relatively carefree state before the pregnancy occurred.

GAY AND LESBIAN STUDENTS

Gay and lesbian students exist on all campuses, but the degree of their visibility, organization, and politicization will vary considerably. These differences, in turn, will affect those students who seek therapy and possibly the problems they present. Obviously, gay and lesbian students must cope with the same developmental tasks as do other students, but, in addition, they must establish and integrate a sexual orientation which may or may not be clear. Thus, some individuals may have no doubts about their homosexual orientation, and it is not unusual for students to say that they have "always known they were gay." There are other students, however, who are aware of both homosexual and heterosexual impulses. While they may accept behavior that involves sexual encounters with both sexes, they are confused about how these feelings relate to the choice of a primary relationship. Still another group may have religious or moral objections to being gay, and as a result seek therapy in the hope that it may help them to achieve a satisfactory heterosexual life. There are also homosexually oriented students who seek therapy for concerns that are not related to sexual orientation; indeed, during a course of brief therapy, sexuality may never be mentioned (Dillon, 1986). Some gay men seek help to enable them to establish a stable love relationship as opposed to brief encounters.

The following illustrates a student who was troubled by his sexual orientation and by his promiscuity.

Michael, a junior, was beset by anxiety and depression toward the end of the year for reasons that were not totally clear. A brilliant student, he still developed anxiety during exam periods although there was no realistic reason for his anxiety state. A dean suggested that he come to the mental health service, but his decision to follow the suggestion occurred only after talking with a friend who had been in therapy. He initially presented his problem in a manner that did not seem to warrant the amount of anxiety he described, and in response to a general question from the therapist he rather reluctantly stated that he thought the anxiety also related to his homosexual concerns.

He went on to say that he had never been able to discuss these concerns with anyone and felt very isolated as a result. He described feeling disgusted in dormitory bull sessions when other guys described their sexual adventures, although he gets along well with women socially.

Although he always felt that he was "different," overt homosexual activity did not begin until he was 18, and consisted of brief encounters. He had not been involved in a sustained relationship and had begun to feel that a homosexual relationship could not be emotionally satisfying. He described guilt about his homosexual activities and wished that he could transform his friendships with women into a sexualized experience.

He was seen briefly in treatment, and it appeared that the opportunity to discuss his homosexual feelings and his conflict about them was beneficial. Although the precise relationship did not become clear, there did seem to be some connection between his exam anxiety and his sexual feelings. Therapy helped sufficiently so that he was able to study effectively, but it did not resolve his sexual conflicts. It was later learned that he had again sought treatment following his graduation.

This vignette comes from the era prior to the known existence of AIDS. If the same student were in therapy at any time after 1983, the therapist would have found a way to explore further the student's activity or to discuss the hazards involved, depending on what the student described.

Some gay students feel that they would prefer to work with a therapist who is openly gay, because no matter what the therapist claims, such students are suspicious that a therapist, presumably heterosexual, will be critical of their homosexuality. Most, however, are willing to work with any therapist who is nonjudgmental and accepting of the student's homosexual orientation. In confirming this acceptance, therefore, it is important for the therapist to be careful about asking questions that can be "heard" by the student as suggesting or urging heterosexual behavior. As gay students become more open about their orientation, they may become less conflicted about seeking therapy for whatever reason, but they may also be more influenced by political positions of the campus gay organization (Henderson, 1984).

Currently, of course, a not infrequent reason for seeking therapy is concern about AIDS. This concern can range from anxiety about a past encounter that in retrospect may seem risky, which in turn raises the question whether an antibody test is advisable, to the panic that is kindled when a diagnosis of AIDS has been made. In between are anxieties that may accompany a positive HIV test, a diagnosis of ARC, or a friend developing AIDS (Keeling, 1989).

> Dennis, a junior, had always done well socially and academically. He was happy about being in his first long-term relationship, but anxious and despondent about the feeling that he should come out to his family. He came to the health service after experiencing marked fatigue for two weeks, which didn't seem to be getting better. The doctor at the health service made a diagnosis of EB viral infection. When he could not be dissuaded from his growing obsession that he might have AIDS, he was referred for psychiatric assistance. Although he was somewhat reassured by a negative HIV titer, it appeared that his anxiety related in part to his relationship with his family and his concern about their anticipated reactions to his revelation of being gay. He expressed some ambivalence about being gay, and also apprehension about his vulnerability to loss as his relationship with his lover became more committed and intense. He began to feel that he had much more control of his life after a few therapy sessions. He thought through what he would tell his parents at an appropriate time in the future. He felt less ambivalence about himself and his lover, and he became involved in AIDS education and prevention activities. He was referred to a gay and lesbian support group for continuing support and help.

The therapeutic work helped the student to clarify some confusion in his feelings and to think out in a neutral atmosphere how he could meet his anxiety about his family.

FOREIGN STUDENTS

Foreign students offer special challenges to the therapist (Martinez et al., 1989; Reifler, 1988; Zwingmann & Gunn, 1983). Most lack their usual social supports, must adjust to a new culture, language, and food, and consequently may come to feel isolated and trapped. They frequently seek help for the relief of physical symptoms that are without demonstrable organic basis, but often it is difficult to convince them that their symptoms are manifestations of psychological distress.

> Reiko, a senior, was admitted to the infirmary following a suicide attempt. She had ingested some pills the week before she was due to depart for Japan. She was mute and lay in her bed with tears running down her face. It was very difficult to get her to talk. She looked miserable, and one felt the presence of grief and a silent appeal for help. Eventually, it emerged that Reiko's family was pressuring her to return home. She wanted to stay in the United States where she felt free and fulfilled and dreaded the thought of returning to the family-oriented women's society at home. She had hoped to pursue a business career, but felt trapped and unable to resist her family's directive to return home. On the surface her dilemma involved the clear clash of differing cultural expectations. No information is available to determine whether or not there was further underlying psychopathology.

Foreign students are frequently unsure what behavior is appropriate and have difficulty "reading" fellow students because of unfamiliarity with culturally based signals. This difficulty can lead to excessive caution in pursuing relationships, rejection because of culturally inappropriate behavior, or poor choice of a potential romantic partner. The therapist also faces the problem of "reading" the foreign student and assessing what part of the problem is culturally normal and what is in fact a symptom. Labeling culturally accepted behavior as pathology is countertherapeutic, but not recognizing personal pain or serious pathology is equally unhelpful. If the therapist is straightforward with the student about the dilemma, the student feels like a respected collaborator, and the chances of sorting out which is which are improved.

Although the student described in the next vignette was not

foreign born, some of the cultural issues of a "first generation" transplant pose comparable dilemmas.

Anna was an attractive young woman, a sophomore of Greek extraction, with large dark eyes and long black hair. She came to the clinic upset about the recent break-up with a boyfriend she had been dating for six months. She claimed he had dropped her abruptly for another woman. For one month she grieved the loss with the help of two visits with her therapist. At that point she said she felt ready to stop. During these sessions, however, the therapist learned that Anna phoned her mother almost daily, and so was reluctant to terminate, believing that Anna's behavior represented poor separation from her family and that more help was needed. This was not stated explicitly and Anna compliantly kept appointments. A few weeks later the therapist inadvertently learned from another conversation that sons and daughters of all ages in this Greek community call family constantly; that this behavior is usual or normal for this cultural group and not a sign, as the therapist assumed (despite lack of other clinical evidence), of poor individuation. With the therapist's improved understanding, the student's wish to terminate was respected.

At times foreign students present with serious psychopathology, and it appears that this may be an intuitive way of achieving a desired end without breaching cultural norms.

Li was a freshman who had spent the last two years of high school in the United States. He was brought to the hospital by his roommates in a mute and apparently catatonic state. After several days in the hospital and several unsuccessful attempts to communicate with him, his parents in Taiwan were called to come and get him. After this step was taken, it emerged that Li did not want to continue in college without some time out between high school and college, and felt unhappy with the family he was living with in the United States. He did not dare express this wish overtly to his parents. His muteness, mostly unconsciously determined, brought about the required outcome without his ever directly defying his parents.

STUDENTS RETURNING FROM A LEAVE OF ABSENCE

Students often take time off during the college years. This may result from dissatisfaction with college, academic failure, inability to move on from a broken romance, disciplinary issues, or emotional problems. It can also reflect a simple wish to do something else for a while: either to get away in order to find a sense of purpose, or to pursue some particular interest or activity outside of college. Almost all these students finish college eventually and feel that the time away was useful (Johnson & Schwartz, 1989).

Assuming that students are not coerced into returning prematurely, the return after a leave is usually a positive experience. Many students become clearer about goals; they feel refreshed and are ready to "go for it"; they have learned something about themselves. Conversely, returning students may discover that former friends are no longer there or have moved on to new relationships. Those students who did not leave under happy circumstances have the greatest reentry problems. College may be associated with painful memories, and they may fear a recurrence of their difficulties. Such students may require help in order to cope with their return.

Walter withdrew in the middle of his senior year. He had suffered a rather severe psychotic episode that had developed gradually over a period of six months. Shortly after withdrawal, he was admitted to a psychiatric hospital. In time, with the help of psychotropic medication and supportive psychotherapy, the psychosis remitted, and he was discharged to a halfway house. He obtained a volunteer job, continued in psychotherapy, gradually tapered his medication, and after a year applied for readmission. Just prior to returning, he attended summer school and managed creditably, so he was readmitted with the plan that he would continue to work with his outpatient psychiatrist at home.

Within a month, however, he was noted to be almost incoherent and was brought to the health service by a dean, who felt that he was seriously impaired. Medication was restarted, and, as he improved, it became clear that his reentry had been adversely affected by the fact that all his friends, whom he had counted on for support, had graduated, and he felt isolated and lonely in the dormitory. Although he was anxious to graduate, he also felt uncertain about his future; his illness had shaken his confidence and raised internal doubts about his abilities. All these concerns apparently joined to precipitate the relapse. With supportive psychotherapy and careful monitoring of his medications, he managed to catch up in his classwork and began to regain some confidence. He established a limited support network and, like many others with psychiatric illnesses, he was able to graduate from college and go on to the next phase of his life.

FURTHER IMPLICATIONS

Every student-patient is a unique individual. This is a basic tenet for psychotherapists and counselors and is especially important to remember in the college context because there is inevitably a rich admixture among students of different psychosocial, ethnic, and economic backgrounds. Similarly, age, sex, and sexual orientation affect the ways in which students experience whatever life crises propel them toward therapy.

The groups we have discussed and vignettes presented illustrate just some of the unique features that may characterize certain students, and that must be taken into consideration over and above the particular complaints, history, and developmental issues that any given student presents.

Ideally, therapists need to recognize the special attributes of each student in order to better understand him or her. It is important in this regard not to overemphasize any single characteristic of the student, as if this forms the totality of the student's identity. On the other hand, neglecting some special attribute of the student can interfere with the therapist's understanding of how this attribute defines an aspect of the student's identity.

A sensitive and perceptive student may respond by wondering whether the therapist is hiding negative, judgmental or prejudicial feelings. It is important for therapists to learn to listen to students, to ask if they don't understand, and to avoid making assumptions about the student based on preconceived stereotypes. Certain formulations may be true in general, but may not necessarily apply to a particular student. It is best to approach the student as a collaborator in testing the accuracy of the therapist's perceptions; this can often be accomplished by noting the student's response to formulations or interpretations. We enlist the student's help in clarifying how a particular feature of the student's identity may or may not be involved in the difficulties for which help is sought.

Lastly, respecting the student's sense of self-worth is essential. Because self-worth is related to the individual's perception of self in a particular world of origin and how that perception can be integrated with a similar self-perception in the college environment, it is crucial for the therapist not to ignore differences, but rather to acknowledge them, and to attempt to know and understand the whole person.

8
SOME AFTERTHOUGHTS

Our report has been primarily concerned with the conduct of psychotherapy for college students. Accordingly, it is directed toward mental health professionals. Nevertheless, it may be helpful not only to that specialized group, but to college administrators and faculty as well. In particular, it provides information about the expectable psychological development of college students as well as the problems and illnesses they may experience during this four-year period. Furthermore, it provides guidelines that a college might follow in designing an appropriate psychiatric service for students.

Currently, we have relatively little systematic research data about the academic and nonacademic lives of college students. During the 1950s and 1960s, several large scale studies of the emotional and intellectual development of college students were undertaken and completed. No such longitudinal studies have been made since 1970. The one major source of knowledge about college students is the annual nationwide survey of entering freshmen conducted annually by the Higher Education Research Institute, Graduate School of Education, University of California at Los Angeles. Faculty and administrators, however, are deprived of detailed information about students' reactions after they enter college, namely, their manifold responses to the classroom; to life in the dorms, apartments, and fraternity or sorority houses; and in the case of commuting students, to life off campus and at home. The knowledge acquired by psychotherapists and counselors is an underused resource, partly because of confidentiality, and partly because therapists are rarely asked for the kind of aggregate data that could be presented without breaching confidentiality.

The present report describes in some detail not just problems that particular students or groups of students face, but also the situations that stimulate, challenge, or threaten students. Choosing a major, navigating an advanced course, responding to a difficult professor, interacting with and learning from peers, establishing autonomy vis-à-vis one's family and friends, all pose challenges, which can be opportunities for growth as well as occasions for calamity. The report distinguishes how freshman year problems differ from sophomore year difficulties and again from those of the junior and senior years. Usually administrators and faculty are aware of these differences in a general way, but the report provides a detailed account of how the routine academic tasks interact with aspects of maturing.

Some may say that the data of this report are derived from "sick" and, therefore, atypical students. But evidence accumulated over several decades, both in longitudinal research on college students and from clinical experience, shows that students who seek out psychiatric or psychological services are representative of the total student body (Frank & Kirk, 1976; King, 1968). The difference seems to be less in the nature of the problems and more in the fact that some students have greater ability to articulate their difficulties and more willingness to acknowledge them. Some studies (Ellis, 1968) even indicate that more psychologically mature students are the ones who are more likely to seek out psychiatric services. Of course, some users of the college's mental health services exhibit more severe pathology. It is well to recognize, however, that other students who do not use these services may nonetheless be afflicted with serious underlying disturbance that they manage to live with or disguise, or are already in treatment off campus.

The lessons from the mental health service are particularly instructive for those administrators and faculty who wish to learn more about the conditions under which student learning is possible. These lessons provide knowledge of the vulnerabilities of student self-esteem, of student needs for encouragement, and of the beneficial outcome when learning is enhanced by appropriate personal teacher-student relationships. The student's striving for autonomy and intellectual mastery can be thwarted by a number of factors: by the teacher's approach in the classroom, by curricular arrangements that lead to intellectual overfeeding or underfeeding, by residential situations, and by peer pressures that undercut intellectual and emotional growth.

Good psychotherapy is an important aid in the individualization of student learning. To be effective, the therapist must recognize the idiosyncratic complexity of students and must have a sense of their individual strivings for autonomy, mastery, and connectedness. These impulses can be in balance or in conflict with each other. When conflict predominates, psychotherapy can improve the learning process. Students in many classrooms are seldom addressed as individuals, much less as individual thinkers. This lack of individuation can make the cultivation of their intellectual powers difficult. Psychotherapy, confronting students at the intersection of their intellectual, occupational, and emotional capacities, attitudes, and aspirations, becomes an instrument for growth.

In thinking about an appropriate student mental health service, one must first realize that college psychiatry is not primarily a service to the deviant or abnormal. Experience shows that when good psychotherapeutic services are available, 25% or more of a given class will seek help during the four years of college (Reifler & Liptzin, 1969). Among them are many students distinguished by special intellectual talents and academic achievements. The benefits of the service are not confined to the "patients" alone but affect other students as well. Wrestling with the crises and challenges in one's own life gives people special insights and ways of looking at problems. They can then communicate some of what they have learned to fellow students who may not themselves seek out therapy. Also, having a resource available that can provide a resolution for troubling problems can limit the spread of adverse effects from such problems within the college community.

The availability of good psychotherapeutic help can positively affect attitudes about sex and drinking, as well as responses to the intellectual and social expectations of the college, to crises in relationships, and to traumatic events, such as the death of a parent or sibling. This report, therefore, constitutes a challenge to administrators and concerned faculty to pay greater attention to the psychological conditions that make effective learning possible. Psychotherapy, as conceived in this report, can play an important role in facilitating education.

REFERENCES

Arnstein, R.L. (1984). Young adulthood: Stages of maturity. In D. Offer & M. Sabshin (Eds.), *Normality and the life cycle* (pp. 108–145). New York: Basic Books.

Arnstein, R.L. (1989). A student mental health service as a place to work: What is its role in the university and how does it affect the therapeutic effort? Presentation at Tavistock Symposium, London.

Binder, J.L., Henry, W.P., & Strupp, H.H. (1987). An appraisal of selection criteria for dynamic psychotherapies and implications for setting time limits, *Psychiatry, 50*, 154–166.

Blaine, G.B. (1964). Divided loyalties: The college therapist's responsibility to the student, the university and the parents, *American Journal of Orthopsychiatry, 34*, 481–485.

Blos, P. (1962). *On adolescence: A psychoanalytic interpretation.* New York: Free Press.

Blos, P. (1979). *The adolescent passage.* New York: International Universities Press.

Blos, P. (1980). Modifications in the traditional psychoanalytic theory of female adolescent development. In S.C. Feinstein & P.L. Giovacchini (Eds.), *Adolescent psychiatry* (Vol. 8, pp. 8–24). Chicago: University of Chicago Press.

Blotcky, M. & Looney, J.C. (1980). Normal Female and Male Adolescent Psychological Development: An Overview of Theory and Research. In S.C. Feinstein & P.L. Giovacchini (Eds.), *Adolescent psychiatry* (Vol. 8, pp. 184–189). Chicago: University of Chicago Press.

Bryt, A. (1979). Developmental tasks in adolescence. In S.C. Feinstein & P.L. Giovacchini (Eds.), *Adolescent psychiatry* (Vol. 7, pp. 136–146). Chicago: University of Chicago Press.

Buhler C. (1968). The course of human life as psychological problem. *Human Development, 11*, 184–200.

Burns, W.D., Sloan, D.C., & Sloan, B.C. (Eds.) (1987). Students, alcohol and college health: A special issue. *Journal of American College Health, 36*(2).

Davanloo, H. (1978). *Basic principles and techniques in short-term dynamic psychotherapy.* New York: Spectrum.

D'Andrea, V.J. (1987). Peer counseling in colleges and universities: A developmental viewpoint, *Journal of College Student Psychotherapy, 1*, 39–55.

Dillon, C. (1986). Preparing college health professionals to deliver gay affirmative services. *Journal of American College Health, 35*, 36–40.

Dorosin, D., Gibbs, J., & Kaplan, L. (1976). Very brief interventions: A pilot evaluation. *Journal of the American College Health Association, 24*, 191–194.

Ehrhart, J.K. & Sandler, B.R. (1985). *Campus gang rape: Party games?* Pamphlet by the Project on the Status and Education of Women, Association of American Colleges.

Ellis, V. (1968). Students who seek psychiatric help. In J. Katz, H.A. Korn, V. Ellis, P. Madison, S. Singer, M.M. Lozoff, M.M. Levin, & N. Sanford (Eds.), *No time for youth.* San Francisco: Jossey-Bass.

Erikson, E.H. (1945). Childhood and tradition in two American Indian tribes. *Psychoanalytic study of the child, 1*, 319–350.

Erikson, E.H. (1946). Ego development and historical change. *Psychoanalytic Study of the Child, 2*, 359–397.

Erikson, E.H. (1950). *Childhood and society.* New York: W.W. Norton.

Erikson, E.H. (1956). The problem of ego identity. *Journal of the American Psychoanalytic Association, 4*, 56–122.

Faigel, H.C. (1985). When the learning disabled go to college. *Journal of American College Health, 34*, 18–22.

Frank, A.C. & Kirk, B.A. (1976). Counseling center and psychiatric service: Who uses each? What happens? *Journal of the American College Health Association, 24*, 221–226.

Freed, B.F. (1987). Exemptions from the foreign language requirement: A review of recent literature, problems, and policy. *ADFL Bulletin, 18*, 13–17.

Gajar, A.H. (1987). Foreign language learning disabilities: The identification of predictive and diagnostic variables. *Journal of Learning Disabilities, 20*, 327–330.

Gilligan, C. (1982). *In a different voice: Psychological theory and women's development.* Cambridge: Harvard University Press.

Grayson, P.A. (1986). Mental health confidentiality on the small campus. *Journal of American College Health, 34*, 187–191.

Group for the Advancement of Psychiatry. (1965). *Sex and the college student.* New York: Group for the Advancement of Psychiatry.

Group for the Advancement of Psychiatry. (1975). *The educated woman: Prospects and problems.* New York: Group for the Advancement of Psychiatry.

Group for the Advancement of Psychiatry. (1983). *Friends and lovers in the college years.* New York: Group for the Advancement of Psychiatry.

Haggerty, J., Baldwin, B.A.,& Liptzin, M.B. (1980). Very brief interventions in college mental health. *Journal of the American College Health Association, 28*, 326–329.

Hartmann, H. (1958). *Ego psychology and the problem of adaptation.* New York: International Universities Press.

Hartmann, H. (1960). *Psychoanalysis and moral values*. New York: International Universities Press.

Heath, R. (1979). *Princeton retrospectives*. Princeton, NJ: Class of 1954, Princeton University.

Heilbrun, C. (1988). *Writing a woman's life*. Ballantine: New York.

Henderson, A.F. (1984). Homosexuality in the college years: Developmental differences between men and women. *Journal of American College Health, 32*, 216–219.

Higgins, G.C. (1989). Sexual problems. In P.A. Grayson & K. Cauley (Eds.), *College psychotherapy*. New York: Guilford Press.

Johnson, E.A. & Schwartz, A.J. (1989). Returning students. In P.A. Grayson & K. Cauley (Eds.), *College Psychotherapy* (pp. 316–331). New York: Guilford Press.

Josselson, R. (1987). Identity diffusion: A long-term follow-up. In S.C. Feinstein & P.L. Giovacchini (Eds.), *Adolescent psychiatry* (Vol. 14, pp. 230–258). Chicago: University of Chicago Press.

Katz, J., Korn, H.A., Ellis, V., Madison, P., Singer, S., Lozoff, M.M., Levin, M.M., & Sanford, N. (1968). *No time for youth*, San Francisco: Jossey-Bass.

Keeling, R.P. (1989). AIDS. in P.A. Grayson & K. Cauley (Eds.), *College psychotherapy* (pp. 261–273). New York: Guilford Press.

King, S. (1968). Characteristics of students seeking psychiatric help. *Journal of the American College Health Association, 17*, 150–156.

Koop, E. (1988, May 25) Surgeon General's press conference on abortion. *New York Times*.

Lee, R.M. (1989). Anorexia nervosa and bulimia nervosa. In P.A. Grayson & K. Cauley (Eds.), *College psychotherapy*. New York: Guilford Press.

Levinson, D.J., Darrow, C.N., Klein, E.B., Levinson, M.H., & McKee, B. (1978). *The seasons of a man's life*. New York: Knopf.

Lidz, T. (1968). *The person*. New York: Basic Books.

Malamuth, N.M. (1984). Aggression against women: Cultural and individual cases. In N.M. Malamuth & E. Donnerstein (Eds.), *Pornography and sexual aggression* (pp. 19–52). Orlando, FL: Academic Press.

Malan, D.H. (1976). *The frontier of brief psychotherapy*. New York: Plenum Medical Book Co.

Mann, J. (1973). *Time-limited psychotherapy*. Cambridge, MA: Harvard University Press.

Marsh. K. (1989). Personal communication.

Martinez, A.M., Huang, K.H.C., Johnson, S.D., Jr., & Edwards, S., Jr. (1989). Ethnic and international students. In P.A. Grayson & K. Cauley (Eds.), *College psychotherapy* (pp. 298–315). New York: Guilford Press.

Medalie, J.D. (1987). Psychotherapy referral as a therapeutic goal of college counseling. *Journal of College Student Psychotherapy, 1*, 83–103.

Meilman, P.W., & Gaylor, M.S. (1989). Substance abuse. In P.A. Grayson & K. Cauley (Eds.), *College psychotherapy*. New York: Guilford Press.

Miller, E.K., & Cabell, E.A. (1989). Mental health and academic competence: Assistance for learning disabled students, *Journal of College Student Psychotherapy, 4*, 65–81.

Miller, J.B. (1976). *Toward a new psychology of women.* Boston: Beacon Press.

Moorman, J.C., Urbach, J., & Ross, D. (1984). Guidelines for consultation with university personnel in student psychiatric emergencies. *Journal of American College Health, 33,* 91–94.

Neugarten, B.L. (1969). Continuities and discontinuities of psychological issues in adult life. *Human Development, 12,* 121–130.

Neugarten, B.L. (1971). Introduction to the symposium: Models and methods for the study of the life cycle. *Human Development, 14,* 81–86.

Offer, D., & Offer, J.B. (1975). *From teenage to young manhood: A psychological study.* New York: Basic Books.

Perry, W. (1968). *Forms of intellectual and ethical development in the college years.* New York: Holt, Rinehart & Winston.

Pfeffer, C.R. (1988). Clinical dilemmas in the prevention of adolescent suicidal behavior. In S. Feinstein (Ed.), *Adolescent psychiatry* (Vol. 15, pp. 407–421). Chicago: University of Chicago Press.

Reifler, C.B. (Ed.) (1988). International student health: A social issue. *Journal of American College Health, 36,* 303–358.

Reifler, C.B., & Liptzin, M.B. (1969). Epidemiological studies of college mental health. *Archives of General Psychiatry, 20,* 528–540.

Ritvo, S. (1976). Adolescent to woman. *Journal of the American Psychoanalytic Association, 24,* 127–139.

Salovey, P., D'Andrea, V.J. (1984). A survey of campus peer counseling activities. *Journal of American College Health, 32,* 262–265.

Schafer, R. (1973). Problems in Freud's psychology of women. *Journal of the American Psychoanalytic Association, 22,* 459–486.

Schneidman, E. (1986). Some essentials of suicide and some implications for response. In A. Roy (Ed.), *Suicide.* Baltimore: Williams & Wilkins.

Schwartz, A.J., & Reifler, C.B. (1984). Quantitative aspects of college mental health: Usage rates, prevalence and incidence. *Psychiatric Annals, 14,* 681–688.

Sifneos, P.E. (1979). *Short-term psychotherapy: Evaluation and technique.* New York: Plenum Medical Book Co.

Steinfirst, J.L., Cowell, S.A., Presley, B.A., Reifler, C.B. (1985). Vending machines and the self-care concept. *Journal of American College Health, 34,* 37–39.

Ursano, R.J., & Hales, R.E. (1986). A review of brief individual psychotherapies. *American Journal of Psychiatry, 143,* 1507–1517.

Vaillant, G. (1977). *Adaptation to life.* Boston: Little, Brown.

Whitaker, L.C. (1989). Suicide and other crises. In P.A. Grayson & K. Cauley, (Eds.), *College psychotherapy,* New York: Guilford Press.

Wittenberg, R. (1968). *Postadolescence,* New York: Grune & Stratton.

Yale University Health Service. (1988). *Sexual assault and the Yale student.* New Haven: Yale University Printing Service.

Yegedis, B.L. (1986). Date rape and other forced sexual encounters among college students. *Journal of Sex Education and Therapy, 12,* 51–54.

Zwingman, C.A.A. & Gunn, A.D.G. (1983). Uprooting and health psychosocial problems of students from abroad. World Health Organization/ MNH 83.8.

GAP COMMITTEES AND MEMBERSHIP

COMMITTEE ON ADOLESCENCE
Warren J. Gadpaille, Denver, CO, Chairperson
Hector R. Bird, New York, NY
Ian A. Canino, New York, NY
Michael G. Kalogerakis, New York, NY
Paulina F. Kernberg, New York, NY
Clarice J. Kestenbaum, New York, NY
Richard C. Marohn, Chicago, IL
Silvio J. Onesti, Jr., Belmont, MA

COMMITTEE ON AGING
Gene D. Cohen, Washington, DC, Chairperson
Eric D. Caine, Rochester, NY
Charles M. Gaitz, Houston, TX
Ira R. Katz, Philadelphia, PA
Andrew F. Leuchter, Los Angeles, CA
Gabe J. Maletta, Minneapolis, MN
Robert J. Nathan, Philadelphia, PA
George H. Pollock, Chicago, IL
Kenneth M. Sakauye, New Orleans, LA
Charles A. Shamoian, Larchmont, NY
F. Conyers Thompson, Jr., Atlanta, GA

COMMITTEE ON ALCOHOLISM AND THE ADDICTIONS
Joseph Westermeyer, Minneapolis, MN, Chairperson
Margaret H. Bean-Bayog, Lexington, MA
Susan J. Blumenthal, Washington, DC
Richard J. Frances, Newark, NJ
Marc Galanter, New York, NY
Edward J. Khantzian, Haverhill, MA
Earl A. Loomis, Jr., Augusta, GA
Sheldon I. Miller, Newark, NJ
Robert B. Millman, New York, NY
Steven M. Mirin, Westwood, MA
Edgar P. Nace, Dallas, TX
Norman L. Paul, Lexington, MA
Peter Steinglass, Washington, DC
John S. Tamerin, Greenwich, CT

COMMITTEE ON CHILD PSYCHIATRY
Peter E. Tanguay, Los Angeles, CA, Chairperson
James M. Bell, Canaan, NY
Harlow Donald Dunton, New York, NY
Joseph Fischhoff, Detroit, MI
Joseph M. Green, Madison, WI
John F. McDermott, Jr., Honolulu, HI
David A. Mrazek, Denver, CO
Cynthia R. Pfeffer, White Plains, NY
John Schowalter, New Haven, CT
Theodore Shapiro, New York, NY
Leonore Terr, San Francisco, CA

COMMITTEE ON CULTURAL
PSYCHIATRY
Ezra E.H. Griffith, New Haven, CT,
  Chairperson
Edward F. Foulks, New Orleans, LA
Redro Ruiz, Houston, TX
Ronald M. Wintrob, Providence, RI
Joe Yamamoto, Los Angeles, CA

COMMITTEE ON THE FAMILY
Herta A. Guttman, Montreal, PQ,
  Chairperson
W. Robert Beavers, Dallas, TX
Ellen M. Berman, Merrion, PA
Lee Combrinck-Graham, Evanston,
  IL
Ira D. Glick, New York, NY
Frederick Gottlieb, Los Angeles, CA
Henry U. Grunebaum, Cambridge,
  MA
Ann L. Price, Hartford, CT
Lyman C. Wynne, Rochester, NY

COMMITTEE ON GOVERNMENTAL
AGENCIES
Roger Peele, Washington, DC,
  Chairperson
Mark Blotcky, Dallas, TX
James P. Cattell, San Diego, CA
Thomas L. Clannon, San Francisco,
  CA
Naomi Heller, Washington, DC
John P.D. Shemo, Charlottesville, VA
William W. Van Stone, Palo Alto,
  CA

COMMITTEE ON HANDICAPS
William H. Sack, Portland, OR,
  Chairperson
Norman R. Bernstein, Cambridge,
  MA
Meyer S. Gunther, Wilmette, IL
Betty J. Pfefferbaum, Houston, TX
William A. Sonis, Philadelphia, PA
Margaret L. Stuber, Los Angeles, CA

George Tarjan, Los Angeles, CA
Thomas G. Webster, Washington,
  DC
Henry H. Work, Bethesda, MD

COMMITTEE ON HUMAN SEXUALITY
Bertram H. Schaffner, New York,
  NY, Chairperson
Paul L. Adams, Galveston, TX
Johanna A. Hoffman, Scottsdale, AZ
Joan A. Lang, Galveston, TX
Stuart E. Nichols, New York, NY
Harris B. Peck, New Rochelle, NY
John P. Spiegel, Waltham, MA
Terry S. Stein, East Lansing, MI

COMMITTEE ON INTERNATIONAL
RELATIONS
Vamik D. Volkan, Charlottesville,
  VA, Chairperson
Robert M. Dorn, El Macero, CA
John S. Kafka, Washington, DC
Otto F. Kernberg, White Plains, NY
John E. Mack, Chestnut Hill, MA
Peter A. Olsson, Houston, TX
Rita R. Rogers, Palos Verdes Estates,
  CA
Stephen B. Shanfield, San Antonio,
  TX

COMMITTEE ON MEDICAL
EDUCATION
Stephen C. Scheiber, Deerfield, IL,
  Chairperson
Charles M. Culver, Hanover, NH
Steven L. Dubovsky, Denver, CO
Saul I. Harrison, Torrance, CA
David R. Hawkins, Chicago, IL
Harold I. Lief, Philadelphia, PA
Carol Nadelson, Boston, MA
Carolyn B. Robinowitz, Washington,
  DC
Sidney L. Werkman, Washington,
  DC
Veva H. Zimmerman, New York,
  NY

David B. Robbins, Chappaqua, NY
Jay B. Rohrlich, New York, NY
Clarence J. Rowe, St. Paul, MN
Jeffrey L. Speller, Cambridge, MA

COMMITTEE ON PSYCHOPATHOLOGY
David A. Adler, Boston, MA,
  Chairperson
Jeffrey Berlant, Summit, NJ
John P. Docherty, Nashua, NH
Robert A. Dorwart, Cambridge, MA
Robert E. Drake, Hanover, NH
James M. Ellison, Watertown, MA
Howard H. Goldman, Potomac, MD
Anthony F. Lehman, Baltimore, MD
Kathleen A. Pajer, Pittsburgh, PA
Samuel G. Siris, Glen Oaks, NY

COMMITTEE ON PUBLIC EDUCATION
Steven E. Katz, New York, NY,
  Chairperson
Jack W. Bonner, III, Asheville, NC
Jeffrey L. Geller, Worchester, MA
Keith H. Johansen, Dallas, TX
Elise K. Richman, Scarsdale, NY
Boris G. Rifkin, Branford, CT
Andrew E. Slaby, Summit, NJ
Robert A. Solow, Los Angeles, CA
Calvin R. Sumner, Buckhannon, WV

COMMITTEE ON RESEARCH
Robert Cancro, New York, NY,
  Chairperson
Jack A. Grebb, New York, NY
John H. Greist, Madison, WI
Jerry M. Lewis, Dallas, TX
John G. Looney, Durham, NC
Sidney Malitz, New York, NY
Zebulon Taintor, New York, NY

COMMITTEE ON SOCIAL ISSUES
Ian E. Alger, New York, NY,
  Chairperson
William R. Beardslee, Waban, MA

Judith H. Gold, Halifax, N.S.
Roderic Gorney, Los Angeles, CA
Martha J. Kirkpatrick, Los Angeles,
  CA
Perry Ottenberg, Philadelphia, PA
Kendon W. Smith, Pearl River, NY

COMMITTEE ON THERAPEUTIC
  CARE
Donald W. Hammersley,
  Washington, DC, Chairperson
Bernard Bandler, Cambridge, MA
Thomas E. Curtis, Chapel Hill, NC
Donald C. Fidler, Morgantown, WV
William B. Hunter, III,
  Albuquerque, NM
Roberto L. Jimenez, San Antonio,
  TX
Milton Kramer, Cincinnati, OH
Theodore Nadelson, Jamaica Plain,
  MA
William W. Richards, Anchorage, AK

COMMITTEE ON THERAPY
Allen D. Rosenblatt, La Jolla, CA,
  Chairperson
Gerald Alder, Boston, MA
Jules R. Bemporad, Boston, MA
Eugene B. Feigelson, Brooklyn, NY
Robert Michels, New York, NY
Andrew P. Morrison, Cambridge,
  MA
William C. Offenkrantz, Carefree,
  AZ

CONTRIBUTING MEMBERS
Gene Abroms, Ardmore, PA
Carlos C. Alden, Jr., Buffalo, NY
Kenneth Z. Altshuler, Dallas, TX
Francis F. Barnes, Washington, DC
Spencer Bayles, Houston, TX
C. Christian Beels, New York, NY
Elissa P. Benedek, Ann Arbor, MI
Sidney Berman, Washington, DC
H. Keith H. Brodie, Durham, NC

Charles M. Bryant, San Francisco,
 CA
Ewald W. Busse, Durham, NC
Robert N. Butler, New York, NY
Eugene M. Caffey, Jr., Bowie, MD
Ian L.W. Clancey, Maitland, Ont.
Sanford I. Cohen, Coral Gables, FL
Paul E. Dietz, Newport Beach, CA
James S. Eaton, Jr., Washington, DC
Lloyd C. Elam, Nashville, TN
Stanley H. Eldred, Belmont, MA
Joseph T. English, New York, NY
Louis C. English, Pomona, NY
Sherman C. Feinstein, Highland
 Park, IL
Archie R. Foley, New York, NY
Sidney Furst, Bronx, NY
Henry J. Gault, Highland Park, IL
Alexander Gralnick, Port Chester,
 NY
Milton Greenblatt, Sylmar, CA
Lawrence F. Greenleigh, Los
 Angeles, CA
Stanley I. Greenspan, Bethesda, MD
Jon E. Gudeman, Milwaukee, WI
Stanley Hammons, Lexington, KY
William Hetznecker, Merion Station,
 PA
J. Cotter Hirschberg, Topeka, KS
Jay Katz, New Haven, CT
James A. Knight, New Orleans, LA
Othilda M. Krug, Cincinnati, OH
Judith Landau-Stanton, Rochester,
 NY
Alan I. Levenson, Tucson, AZ
Ruth W. Lidz, Woodbridge, CT
Orlando B. Lightfoot, Boston, MA
Norman L. Loux, Sellersville, PA
Albert J. Lubin, Woodside, CA
John A. MacLeod, Cincinnati, OH
Charles A. Malone, Barrington, RI
Peter A. Martin, Lake Orion, MI
Ake Mattsson, Charlottesville, VA
Alan A. McLean, Westport, CT
David Mendell, Houston, TX
Roy W. Menninger, Topeka, KS
Mary E. Mercer, Nyack, NY
Derek Miller, Chicago, IL

Richard D. Morrill, Boston, MA
Joseph D. Noshpitz, Washington, DC
Mortimer Ostow, Bronx, NY
Bernard L. Pacella, New York, NY
Herbert Pardes, New York, NY
Marvin E. Perkins, Salem, VA
David N. Ratnavale, Bethesda, MD
Richard E. Renneker, West Los
 Angeles, CA
W. Donald Ross, Cincinnati, OH
Donald J. Scherl, Brooklyn, NY
Charles Shagrass, Philadelphia, PA
Miles F. Shore, Boston, MA
Albert J. Silverman, Ann Arbor, MI
Benson R. Snyder, Cambridge, MA
David A. Soskis, Bala Cynwyd, PA
Jeanne Spurlock, Washington, DC
Brandt F. Steele, Denver, CO
Alan A. Stone, Cambridge, MA
Perry C. Talkington, Dallas, TX
Bryce Templeton, Philadelphia, PA
Prescott W. Thompson, Portland,
 OR
John A. Turner, San Francisco, CA
Gene L. Usdin, New Orleans, LA
Kenneth N. Vogtsberger, San
 Antonio, TX
Andrew S. Watson, Ann Arbor, MI
Joseph B. Wheelwright, Kentfield,
 CA
Robert L. Williams, Houston, TX
Paul Tyler Wilson, Bethesda, MD
Sherwyn M. Woods, Los Angeles,
 CA
Kent A. Zimmerman, Menlo Park,
 CA

LIFE MEMBERS
C. Knight Aldrich, Charlottesville,
 VA
Bernard Bandler, Cambridge, MA
Walter E. Barton, Hartland, VT
Viola W. Bernard, New York, NY
Murray Bowen, Chevy Chase, MD
Henry W. Brosin, Tucson, AZ
John Donnelly, Hartford, CT
Merrill T. Eaton, Omaha, NE

O. Spurgeon English, Narberth, PA
Stephen Fleck, New Haven, CT
Jerome Frank, Baltimore, MD
Robert S. Garber, Longboat, Key, FL
Robert I. Gibson, Towson, MD
Paul E. Huston, Iowa City, IA
Margaret M. Lawrence, Pomona, NY
Jerry M. Lewis, Dallas, TX
Harold I. Lief, Philadelphia, PA
Judd Marmor, Los Angeles, CA
Karl A. Menninger, Topeka, KS
Herbert C. Modlin, Topeka, KS
John C. Nemiah, Hanover, NH
Alexander S. Rogawski, Los Angeles,
  CA
Mabel Ross, Sun City, AZ
Julius Schreiber, Washington, DC
Robert E. Switzer, Dunn Loring, VA
George Tarjan, Los Angeles, CA
Jack A. Wolford, Pittsburgh, PA
Henry H. Work, Bethesda, MD

BOARD OF DIRECTORS

OFFICERS

President
Carolyn B. Robinowitz
Deputy Medical Director
American Psychiatric Association
1400 K Street, N.W.
Washington, DC 20005

President-Elect
Allan Beigel
30 Camino Español
Tucson, AZ 85716

Secretary
Doyle I. Carson
Timberlawn Psychiatric Hospital
P.O. Box 11288
Dallas, TX 75223

Treasurer
Charles B. Wilkinson
2055 Holmes
Kansas City, MO 64108

Board Members
Judith Gold
Harvey L. Ruben
Pedro Ruiz
John Schowalter

Past Presidents

*William C Menninger	1946-51
Jack R. Ewalt	1951-53
Walter E. Barton	1953-55
*Sol W. Ginsburg	1955-57
*Dana L. Farnsworth	1957-59
*Marion E. Kenworthy	1959-61
Henry W. Brosin	1961-63
*Leo H. Bartemeier	1963-65
Robert S. Garber	1965-67
Herbert C. Modlin	1967-69
John Donnelly	1969-71
George Tarjan	1971-73
Judd Marmor	1973-75
John C. Nemiah	1975-77
Jack A. Wolford	1977-79
Robert W. Gibson	1979-81
*Jack Weinberg	1981-82
Henry H. Work	1982-85
Michael R. Zales	1985-87
Jerry M. Lewis	1987-89

PUBLICATIONS BOARD

Chairman
Alexander S. Rogawski
11665 W. Olympic Blvd. #302
Los Angeles, CA 90064

C. Knight Aldrich
Robert L. Arnstein
Judith H. Gold
Milton Kramer
W. Walter Menninger
Robert A. Solow

Consultant
John C. Nemiah

---

*deceased

GAP Reports Published by Brunner/Mazel, Inc.

A Casebook in Psychiatric Ethics, Report #129

Crisis of Adolescence—Teenage Pregnancy: Impact on
Adolescent Development, Report #118

A Family Affair: Helping Families Cope with Mental Illness:
A Guide for the Professions, Report #119

The Family, the Patient, and the Psychiatric Hospital:
Toward a New Model, Report #117

How Old is Old Enough? The Ages of Rights and
Responsibilities, Report #126

Interactive Fit: A Guide to Nonpsychotic Chronic Patients,
Report #121

The Mental Health Professional and the Legal System,
Report #131

Psychiatric Prevention and the Family Life Cycle, Report #127

The Psychiatric Treatment of Alzheimer's Disease, Report #125

Psychiatry and the Mental Health Professionals: New Roles for
Changing Times, Report #122

Psychotherapy with College Students, Report #130

Research and the Complex Causality of the Schizophrenias,
Report #116

Speaking Out for Psychiatry: A Handbook for Involvement
with the Mass Media, Report #124

Suicide and Ethnicity in the United States, Report #128

Teaching Psychotherapy in Contemporary Psychiatric Residency
Training, Report #120

Us and Them: The Psychology of Ethnonationalism,
Report #123